Bethany Irby, Sloane Warren (with knife), and Rene Dellefont
in *The Weird* at Dad's Garage Theatre.

THE WEIRD

A COLLECTION OF SHORT HORROR AND PULP PLAYS

BY ROBERTO AGUIRRE-SACASA

DRAMATISTS
PLAY SERVICE
INC.

2

ACKNOWLEDGMENTS

The plays that make up *The Weird* were first written and performed separately. The earliest, "Morning Becomes Olestra," was premiered by Cherry Red Productions in Washington, DC. The most recent, "Bloody Mary," premiered as part of *The Weird* at Dad's Garage Theatre in Atlanta. "The Ten-Minute Play About Rosemary's Baby" was first produced by SoHo Rep in New York City; "Insect Love" and "Swamp Gothic" were first produced at the Source Theatre in Washington, DC; and "Dinner with the Superfriends" was first produced by the Yale Cabaret in New Haven, Connecticut.

AUTHOR'S NOTE ON STYLE

Each of the short plays in *The Weird* was inspired by different horror movies and/or comic books and/or plays. As much as possible, it would be great if the individual plays were performed in the different styles that reflect their inspiration.

BLOODY MARY was inspired by teen slasher movies like *Halloween* and *Scream*.

INSECT LOVE was loosely inspired by *The Fly* — the original, not the remake — and should play like a 1950s romance/drama, almost.

THE TEN-MINUTE PLAY ABOUT ROSEMARY'S BABY was inspired by the brilliant horror classic directed by Roman Polanski and the absurdist plays of Edward Albee.

The character names in SWAMP GOTHIC allude to characters from the *Swamp Thing* comic book, but the play's style is Southern gothic/overripe Tennessee Williams.

MORNING BECOMES OLESTRA is a *Tales from the Crypt* comic book story for the stage. (And, while I'm thinking of it, M.T. Grave is a horror host cut from the same cloth as the Crypt-Keeper.)

DINNER WITH THE SUPERFRIENDS is a response to Donald Margulies' excellent relationship play *Dinner with Friends* … and the Saturday morning cartoons of my youth.

THE WEIRD received its world premiere at Dad's Garage Theatre (Scott Warren, Artistic Director; Kathryn Colgrove, Managing Director) in Atlanta, Georgia, opening on October 14, 2004. It was directed by Melissa Foulger and Anne Towns; the set and lighting designs were by Elisabeth Cooper; the costume design was by Carrie Duncan; the sound design was by Tom Myers; the special effects were by Justin Welborn; the property design was by Melisa DuBois; the technical director was Jaime Warde; and the stage manager was Leslye Kahn. The cast was as follows:

BEN, BOY, MATTHEW, HAROLD .... Rene Dellefont
LAURIE, GIRL, SUPERGIRL .... Bethany Irby
DR. DeLAMBRE, MAN, ALEC, AXEL .... Wade Tilton
M.T. GRAVE .... Scott Warren
ABIGAIL, WANDA, FRANCES .... Sloane Warren
CAROLINE, WOMAN .... Kathleen Wattis

The short play BLOODY MARY was subsequently performed as part of "Dread Awakening" (produced by The Thursday Problem, Michelle Bossy, Brian Flanagan, and Alana Karpoff) at the 45th Street Theatre in New York City, opening on April 6, 2006. It was directed by Pat Diamond; the set design was by Wilson Chin; the costume design was by Candice Thompson; the lighting design was by Marcus Doshi; the sound design was by Mark Huang, and the production stage manager was Andy Ottoson. The cast was as follows:

LAURIE .... Christianna Nelson
BEN .... Jedadiah Schultz

CHARACTERS

(in speaking order)

BEN TRAMER, an over-sexed, jockish teenager

LAURIE STRODE, an over-sexed, cheerleaderish teenager and Ben's girlfriend

M.T. GRAVE, a horror host

DR. ANDRE DeLAMBRE, an entomologist

CAROLINE, his lab assistant

BOY, a young man, an actor

GIRL, a young woman, his wife

MAN, an old man named Roman Castavet

WOMAN, Minnie, his wife

ALEC ARCANE, a nineteen-year-old Tulane student

ABIGAIL ARCANE, his sister

MATTHEW CABLE, his friend and lover

HAROLD HOGSWORTH, an enormous fat man

WANDA HOGSWORTH, his hot wife

AXEL, a refrigerator repairman (also a vampire)

STAGE MANAGER, a stage manager or an actor playing a stage manager

BIBBO, the ever-loving proprietor of Bibbo's Luncheonette, an older man with two kids

FRANCES KANE, the superheroine formally known as Magneta; her friends call her Frankie

SUPERGIRL, the world's most powerful teen superheroine, one of two survivors of the doomed planet Krypton; her real name is Kara, she looks — and will always look — seventeen

All of the roles in *The Weird* can be played by different actors; but, if you're going to double some of the roles, here's one way that works nicely:

ACTOR ONE plays M.T. Grave.

ACTOR TWO plays Ben, Boy, Alec, Axel, and Bibbo.

ACTOR THREE plays Dr. DeLambre, Man, Matthew, Harold, and the Stage Manager.

ACTOR FOUR plays Laurie, Caroline, Girl, and Supergirl.

ACTOR FIVE plays Woman, Abigail, Wanda, and Frances.

Of course, the roles can be doubled many different ways, depending on the actors cast.

CONTENTS

BLOODY MARY

CHARACTERS

BEN TRAMER, an over-sexed, jockish teenager

LAURIE STRODE, an over-sexed, cheerleaderish teenager and Ben's girlfriend

BLOODY MARY

Total darkness and we hear:

A MAN'S DISEMBODIED VOICE. *(Repeating.)* Bloody Mary,
Bloody Mary,
Bloody Mary,
Bloody Mary,
Bloody Mary —
(A tight spot comes up on a car cruising along a lonely, deserted highway. Night time. Driving is handsome, popular Ben Tramer. Next to him, fixing her lipstick, is his girlfriend, Laurie Strode. They're both looking into the rearview mirror intently — though for different reasons. Still repeating:) — Bloody Mary,
Bloody Mary,
Bloody Mary,
Bloody Mary,
Bloody Mary,
Bloody —
LAURIE. *(Over Ben's recitation.)* Ben —
BEN. — Mary,
Bloody Mary,
Bloody Mary,
Bloody Mary,
Bloody Mary!
(Beat.) Okay, how many was that?
LAURIE. I don't know, I told you — I'm not playing.
BEN. It's supposed to be forty-nine times, right? You're supposed to say it forty-nine times, while looking into a mirror —
LAURIE. A *bathroom* mirror —
BEN. — *any* mirror. And she supposedly appears to you, right? She — like — *materializes.* All covered in blood, right? *(Beat.)* Isn't that

13

how it works? *(Beat.)* Laurie? *(Beat.)* Oh, *c'mon,* Laurie —

LAURIE. Yes, Ben, it's forty-nine times! Jesus! But I'm telling you — it only works when you're, like, twelve — and you have to be at, like, a slumber party. You can't be *driving,* for Christ's sake! You have to be, you know, concentrating.

BEN. In *Candyman* — you ever see the movie *Candyman* with Tony Todd? — you say the word "Candyman" in the mirror, not "Bloody Mary," and it's not forty-nine times, it's, like, three.

LAURIE. *(Bored.)* Fascinating.

BEN. They must've got the idea from Bloody Mary, though, don't you think? From the Bloody Mary game kids play.

LAURIE. *I* never played it.

BEN. I did …

LAURIE. Because you're a ghoul, Ben. *(Pawing him.)* A total — hottie — ghoul.

BEN. … but it never worked.

LAURIE. Well, duh. 'Cause it's a … whattayacallit? Like the guy with the hook? Stalking Lovers' Lane? Or the guy who calls the babysitter from somewhere inside the house? The children's throats already slit? Their sheets sopping blood?

BEN. I believe what you're referring to is/are … urban legends, Laurie.

LAURIE. Right. Urban —

BEN. — Bloody Mary,

Bloody Mary,

Bloody Mary,

Bloody Mary,

Bloody —

LAURIE. Ben — ?

BEN. Scared?

LAURIE. Why would I be scared?

BEN. 'Cause we're driving to Shadow Lake, Laurie. In the middle of the night, in the middle of nowhere. On the anniversary of … *(He looks at her.)* Hey, are you sure you're up for this? 'Cause it's not too late to back out …

LAURIE. We're making a documentary, Ben, not — not — not —

BEN. — a horror *mock*-umentary actually, Laurie, yeah. Based on a mass murder that happened at Shadow Lake ten years ago. Which we are re-creating — dismemberment by dismemberment — at the *real* Shadow Lake. *(He remembers.)* The wholesale slaughter of

14

a group of camp counselors on the site of an ancient Indian burial ground …

LAURIE. I believe the politically correct term now is "Native Indian," okay?

BEN. Camp counselors who were eviscerated by a masked homicidal killer wielding a machete, their bodies never found — the *killer's* body never found …

LAURIE. Which begs the question: "If their bodies were never found, how do you know they were killed with a machete?" *(Beat.)* I mean *really,* Ben.

BEN. You know what I think, Laurie? I think Cedric's still out there …

LAURIE. Who?

BEN. Cedric — the killer — I think he's still out there at Shadow Lake — *under* Shadow Lake …

LAURIE. Come on, Ben.

BEN. No, I'm serious. I think Cedric's underwater — his slowly decomposing corpse, I mean — waiting for … for the *next* group of teenagers and emotionally arrested twenty-somethings to gather at Shadow Lake … on the anniversary of one of the worst mass murders in New Jersey's history …

LAURIE. Stop it, Ben.

BEN. Twelve over-sexed, over-educated, under-employed emotionally arrested twenty-somethings died that terrible, terrible weekend …

LAURIE. Keep talking about this and guess who's not getting any tonight?

BEN. You're scared, Laurie, and — and that's cool. I'm scared by what we're doing, too, a little bit. But you know what? You know what I believe, Laurie? *(Beat.)* I believe it's when we're scared that we feel most alive. When we're feeling terror, pure terror, undiluted, abject horror of something — death, because all fear is fear of death, or mutilation, of our bodies being mutilated, or of pain — at that moment, when the monsters start slithering out from beneath our beds, or the killer's knife catches the moonlight and reflects it back into our eyeballs, or the zombie's grip tightens around our throats, their teeth sinking into our scalp — that's when we're closest to, to, to — ecstasy. Transformation. Transcendence. *(Beat.)* More than when we're having sex, even.

LAURIE. Oh, well, that's — that's fucking *profound,* Ben. Speaking as your girlfriend, that makes me feel really — *really* — great about myself.

BEN. You know what I mean. *(He starts again.)*

Bloody Mary,

Bloody Mary,

Bloody Mary,

Bloody Mary,

Bloody Mary,

Bloody — *(Laurie turns on the radio.)* Oh, come *on*, Laurie. I'm at, like, forty, and you're totally ruining it. *(An old song, like "Mr. Sandman," is playing on the radio.* Laurie's not pleased.)*

LAURIE. God, what station — ?

BEN. *(Stopping her from changing the station.)* No, no, leave it.

LAURIE. Why?

BEN. Look, I'll make you a deal. If you can tell me what horror movie — what *famous* horror movie *which I know you've seen* — uses this song, I'll stop playing Bloody Mary, stop talking about Shadow Lake (though that *is* where we're going), stop — stop everything. *(Beat.)* And I'll even pleasure *you* tonight.

LAURIE. Gimme a hint.

BEN. Okay, but if you *don't* get it — in three guesses — I get to do something very, very scary, okay?

LAURIE. What's my hint, asshole?

BEN. Okay. It stars … Jamie Lee Curtis.

LAURIE. *Halloween.*

BEN. Strike one.

Bloody Mary. (Forty-one.)

LAURIE. Um … um — oh, oh — ahhhh, *Prom Night.*

BEN. A classic — good guess — but no. Strike two.

Bloody Mary. (Forty-two.)

LAURIE. Okay, okay — ! *(She thinks.)* Fuck, fuck me. Um — okay, okay — uh, *The Fog.*

BEN. Very good, Laurie. Jamie Lee Curtis was indeed in that one, too, opposite the ever-luscious Adrienne Barbeau, and after *Halloween,* it's John Carpenter's finest (though most neglected) film, but alas — no. Strike three.

Bloody Mary. (Forty-four.)

LAURIE. Forty-*three.*

BEN. Bloody Mary. (Forty-four.) It's *Halloween 2.*

LAURIE. I said that!

---

* See Special Note on Songs and Recordings on copyright page.

BEN. No, you said *Halloween 1*.

LAURIE. *"2,"* I meant *"2"!*

BEN. You said *"1."*

LAURIE. You are *such* — such a fucking — *film nerd*, Ben, you know that?

BEN. You ever seen *The Twilight Zone* movie, Laurie? You remember its opening sequence? Two guys, driving at night, along a lonely highway like this one —

LAURIE. Ben —

BEN. The first guy says to the second guy, "Hey. You wanna see something scary?"

LAURIE. Stop it, Ben, okay?

BEN. And the first guy, he turns off all the car's lights. Like this. *(Ben turns off the car's lights, plunging everything into darkness.)*

LAURIE. Ben, I'm serious —

BEN. Don't be scared, Laurie, I've been driving this highway since I was sixteen.

LAURIE. Uh, newsflash: You're *seventeen,* asshole!

BEN. I know this road like I know the creases in the palms of my hands. It's all a matter of ... "keeping your cool, of not losing your head." (What's that from — that line? Guess and I'll turn the lights back on.)

LAURIE. I don't know —

BEN. *Creepshow.*

Bloody Mary. (Forty-five.) The guy's buried in sand — on the beach — up to his neck — and the tide's rolling in and he knows he's gonna drown ...

LAURIE. You — you are so *dumped,* you shit!

BEN. Feel your heart racing? Your pulse pounding? Excited, Laurie?

Bloody Mary. (Forty-six.) *(Remember, the old song is still playing.)*

LAURIE. I'm wondering why the fuck I agreed to this fucking weekend in the fucking first place!

BEN. Because our little project's director asked you to be the lead, the Last Girl, the only one of us who makes it to the last reel, whose resourcefulness enables her to face the Unspeakable, the *Evil* — and survive. *(Beat.)* Maybe.

Bloody Mary. (Forty-seven.)

LAURIE. Maybe? Isn't that one of the, like, rules? That the Last Girl *always* survives? I mean, hel-*lo,* for the sequel?

BEN. The final words our intrepid leader said to me, before he and the others took off for Camp Shadow Lake, was this: "Forget everything you know about horror movies, Ben. Formula is not scary. Sometimes the Last Girl dies. Sometimes there is no return to the status quo before the End Credits. And sometimes ... *sometimes,* the scariest monster in the world is the guy sitting next to you in the dark."

LAURIE. *(Scared.)* Ben ...

BEN. Don't be scared, Laurie.
     Bloody Mary. (Forty-eight.)

LAURIE. *(More scared.)* Oh, God, please don't.

BEN. Bloody —

LAURIE. Don't Ben. Don't —

BEN. — Mary. *(Short pause.)* And that's forty-nine. *(Short pause. The song continues to play.)* Now I'm gonna turn the lights back on —

LAURIE. Ben —

BEN. And I promise you that I'm gonna be me, not some monster, and that we won't see Bloody Mary — whoever she is, anyway — in the mirror, okay? I *promise.* And you'll see that the only thing — when all is said and done — that the only thing we have to hold onto sometimes is our fear. *(Beat.)* Okay? *(Beat.)* Okay, Laurie?

LAURIE. I'm scared, Ben.

BEN. There's nothing to be scared of. *(Ben turns on the lights. Laurie has her eyes closed, but everything is fine. Seriously.)* You can open your eyes now, really. *(Laurie does. On the radio, the song is ending, and:)*

RADIO ANNOUNCER. And that was [name of old song] by [group]. Up next — *(Laurie shuts the radio off.)*

LAURIE. That was a really shitty thing to do, Ben, a really shitty thing.

BEN. Oh, come on, I was just goofing with you.

LAURIE. You're such a — such a *ghoul.*

BEN. All right, I'm sorry.

LAURIE. *God!* I totally need a jawbreaker now! *Jesus! (Laurie starts going through her purse.)*

BEN. Hey, get me one too, will you?

LAURIE. Oh, sure. Terrify me and let me get you a jawbreaker, please. *(Laurie drops her purse.)* Fuck me! *(She bends down, out of sight, revealing behind her: a terrifying vision of blood and gore. Bloody Mary sitting in the back seat, her eyes wide. An ominous chord of music*

— like we hear when Michael Myers sits up towards the end of "Halloween." Laurie continues looking through her purse. Slowly, Bloody Mary raises a knife and turns to Ben, who is driving, oblivious.)
BEN. Hey, you all right down there?
LAURIE. *(Still digging.)* — this fucking purse, I can't fucking find — *(Bloody Mary draws back the knife. Sitting up:)* — got 'em! *(Just before Bloody Mary digs the knife into Ben's head: Blackout. A song like Michael Jackson's "Thriller" starts to play … *)*

End of Play

INTERLUDE ONE

After "Bloody Mary" and before "Insect Love": As the song plays, our evening's host, M.T. Grave, sashays on, doing that "zombie dance," if you know what I mean. A few words about M.T. Grave: He's a mess, folks. Looks like a zombie with flaking skin, dirt in his hair and under his fingernails, hollow eyes, a moth- and maggot-eaten olive-green cloak on his shoulders. Like the Crypt-Keeper from HBO's Tales from the Crypt *or the Creep from* Creepshow 1 *and* 2 *but taller. And not a puppet. In any case, after a few beats, the music cuts out, M.T. notices the audience, stops dancing, and starts yapping.*

M.T. GRAVE. *(To audience.)* Ladies and gentlemen … *creeps* and kiddies … *ghouls* and *boils* …

Good evening, and welcome to another installment of *tumescent tales* of *monsters* and *mayhem,* gratuitous *gore* and *lurid* laughs, despicable *devils* and *devastating* drama …

… exactingly exhumed from the *Tomb of Terror* …

… painstakingly pried from the *Vault of Horror* …

… unapologetically unearthed from the *Crypt of Fear* …

… defeatedly dusted off by the author from his *Drawer of Dread* …

A malevolent little menagerie we decided to call … *The Weird,* presented by these slobbering idiots here at *(Insert producing theatre's name.)* …

I'm your host in horror, your guide to the gruesome, your narrator of the nauseating, Morgan Talbot Grave, but you may call me … M.T. Grave. (Because if my producers take such liberties, why shouldn't you?) *(He starts to cackle; there is thunder and lightning. M.T. gets scared.)*

Our evening's first little offering was called "Bloody Mary" for — well — *obvious* reasons. (A little *too* obvious if you ask me …)

Next up is a study of quiet, subtle dread about scientists and

---

* See Special Note on Songs and Recordings on copyright page.

the people who love them. (And, conversely, the people who crush their horrifically deformed heads under two-ton presses …) *(He gestures to the stage behind him.)*

Ladies and gentlemen, kindly turn off your cell phones if you haven't already — and turn your attention to the laboratory of entomologist Andre DeLambre, in a suburb of Paris, France. The year is 1958, the story is …

… *INSECT LOVE! (M.T. GRAVE vanishes as a song like "Tell Him" starts to play.)*

INSECT LOVE

CHARACTERS

DR. ANDRE DeLAMBRE, an entomologist
CAROLINE, his lab assistant

INSECT LOVE

In the theatre's darkness, a hit song from the 1950s, like "Tell Him" by The Exciters, plays for a few moments.* As the music fades, the lights come up to reveal Dr. André DeLambre, a scientist in a white lab coat. He sits hunched over a microscope, working in his lab. Excitedly, he scribbles notes. His young, pretty assistant, Caroline, comes in. The year is 1958. In movie theatres around the world, The Fly, *starring Vincent Price, is playing.*

CAROLINE.   Good morning, Dr. DeLambre. *(Silence.)* I said, "Good morning — "
DR. DeLAMBRE.   Oh. Uh — good morning, Caroline.
CAROLINE.   How was your weekend, Doctor?
DR. DeLAMBRE.   Quiet. Busy. And yours? You look very nice today, by the way. That's a charming blouse.
CAROLINE.   Thank you. It was fine. Thank you for asking.
DR. DeLAMBRE.   Did you have another date with…? I've forgotten his name!
CAROLINE.   Martin. Yes, we went to the movies. We saw *The Fly.* Have you seen it yet, Doctor?
DR. DeLAMBRE.   No.
CAROLINE.   Oh, you should. You'd enjoy it, I think.
DR. DeLAMBRE.   *(Shaking his head.)* No, I don't care much for horror movies. The world around us is crowded with it; horror. On the television, in the newspapers …
CAROLINE.   Oh, but it isn't horror really.
DR. DeLAMBRE.   Science fiction, then.
CAROLINE.   It's a love story, more than anything else. It's about a scientist, like you, who is consumed by his work.
DR. DeLAMBRE.   My work is important. And I am not con-

sumed by it, I am … freed by it.

CAROLINE. Of course, Doctor. *(Dr. DeLambre returns to his microscope.)*

DR. DeLAMBRE. I spent my weekend thinking about eyes, Caroline.

CAROLINE. Whose?

DR. DeLAMBRE. Yours. Your beautiful green —

CAROLINE. Mine?

DR. DeLAMBRE. *(Pointing to what looks like an empty tank.)* And his.

CAROLINE. The fly's?

DR. DeLAMBRE. *(Nods.)* I want you to see something. *(At DeLambre's urging, Caroline goes to the microscope.)* That fly you're looking at … Its eyes register color the same as ours do. More acutely, even. Their sensitivity to light is greater. Their peripheral vision, too. (Which is why we have so much trouble swatting them; they can see us coming from whichever direction.)

CAROLINE. *(As she peers into the microscope.)* They have no lids …

DR. DeLAMBRE. *(Hesitates.)* No. They never close. If we had eyes like that —

CAROLINE. We wouldn't be able to cry, then.

DR. DeLAMBRE. N-no.

CAROLINE. You have beautiful blue-gray eyes, Doctor.

DR. DeLAMBRE. *(Surprised.)* I — *(Mini-beat.)* — thank you.

CAROLINE. I'll type up your notes from over the weekend now.

DR. DeLAMBRE. Please. *(The lights fade as Caroline sits at her desk. New scene: Lights up on Dr. DeLambre. He is hunched over his microscope. Caroline enters.)*

CAROLINE. Good morning, Dr. DeLambre. *(Silence.)* Doctor?

DR. DeLAMBRE. Good morning, Caroline. How was your evening? Did you and Martin — ?

CAROLINE. — Shall I type your notes from yesterday, Doctor?

DR. DeLAMBRE. Please. *(Caroline stands.)* But first …

CAROLINE. Yes, Doctor?

DR. DeLAMBRE. Aren't you going to ask about *my* evening? Aren't you the least bit — ?

CAROLINE. I'm sorry. Of course. How was it, Doctor? Did you work late again?

DR. DeLAMBRE. No, I went to see *The Fly*. At the Palace. And you were right, I *did* enjoy it. I *loved* it, in fact.

CAROLINE. You *loved The Fly*?

DR. DeLAMBRE. Well, not the science fiction of it, no, nor the horror, necessarily, but ... the philosophy behind it, yes. The man's passion for discovery: unconditional. And his wife's devotion to him: also unconditional. Both are noble characters. And both, in the end, are wedded to science. It becomes their lifeline to each other. It becomes the only thing that can save them.

CAROLINE. Yes. It doesn't, but yes.

DR. DeLAMBRE. She shares his world with him. She doesn't understand it all, of course, but she accepts it.

CAROLINE. She has no choice.

DR. DeLAMBRE. She does, though. She could leave him.

CAROLINE. No — *(Mini-beat.)* — she could not, Doctor. *(Dr. DeLambre considers it.)*

DR. DeLAMBRE. No, you're right. *(Lightening the mood.)* Still, she is lovely, the actress, and I wish it had turned out better for the scientist. His head crushed by a newspaper press. *(Smiles.)* For the fly, too.

CAROLINE. Its head crushed by a rock. *(She smiles, too.)* I'll type your notes now, Doctor, yes?

DR. DeLAMBRE. That's fine. *(She stands again.)* But first ... one more thing.

CAROLINE. Yes?

DR. DeLAMBRE. About flies.

CAROLINE. Of course.

DR. DeLAMBRE. Did you know that fly swarms can be controlled with sound?

CAROLINE. How do you mean?

DR. DeLAMBRE. A loud bang, and the swarm disperses. Music, and the swarm sways. The flies follow the song's rhythm, its beat, its tempo. *(Short pause. Carefully:)* One day ... perhaps ... if you'd like me to ... I'll make flies dance for you, Caroline. *(Dr. DeLambre returns to his work. The lights fade as Caroline goes to her typewriter. New scene: Lights up on the empty laboratory. Caroline enters, carrying two brown lunch bags.)*

CAROLINE. Dr. DeLambre? I have our lunches.

DR. DeLAMBRE. *(From offstage, his voice muffled.)* One second, Caroline, I'm — One second. *(Caroline sits down, starts unwrapping her sandwich. Dr. DeLambre enters. He's wearing a sheet over his head.)*

CAROLINE. Doctor, what is that? *(Dr. DeLambre approaches Caroline, vaguely threatening. Creepy, ominous underscoring — like*

27

from the movie The Fly — *plays. Caroline is nonplussed. Dr. DeLambre stands over Caroline, tears the sheet from his head. Horrors! Dr. DeLambre now has the head of a gigantic fly!)*

CAROLINE. I have your lunch, Doctor.

DR. DeLAMBRE. *(Muffled.)* Aren't you frightened?

CAROLINE. I'm sorry?

DR. DeLAMBRE. *(Muffled, repeating himself.)* Aren't you frightened of me?

CAROLINE. I'm sorry, I can't understand what you're saying. *(Caroline resumes eating. Slightly dejected, Dr. DeLambre sits down. After a few moments:)* Aren't you going to eat? *(Silence from the fly. Caroline takes a bite from her sandwich.)* Do you know what this reminds me of? Our sandwiches? *(The fly shakes its head.)* Once, when I was eight, I went to visit my grandmother, in a house at the edge of a swamp. I went with my father. The night we arrived, my grandmother made us sandwiches, like these, for dinner. We ate, and while we were still eating, she stood up and made us come outside with her. As far from the city as we were, there weren't any lights — no street lamps, no other houses, nothing. Just the blackness of the swamp and the black sky, full of stars, above it. "Wait and see," my grandmother said, and we did, we waited, and my father lifted me up to his shoulders, and in the blackness, one tiny green light began to blink. And then another, and then a third, and more. Until the entire swamp was lit up, blinking in unison — a sky of green stars beneath a sky of white ones. They were fireflies. It was the most wonderful thing I'd ever seen. *(Short pause. Dr. DeLambre takes off his mask.)*

DR. DeLAMBRE. One of my students made this mask for me. As a joke. A — prank.

CAROLINE. It's very good. Is it papier mâché?

DR. DeLAMBRE. Caroline, are those fireflies — from your story — are they the reason you want to study insects with me?

CAROLINE. No, Doctor. They're not. *(Slow blackout. New scene: Lights up on Dr. DeLambre. He is not hunched over anything. Plainly, he is waiting for Caroline. He wants to show her something. Caroline enters, carrying books.)*

DR. DeLAMBRE. Good morning, Caroline, may I show you something?

CAROLINE. Of course. Please.

DR. DeLAMBRE. *(Pointing to what appears to be an empty tank.)* I want you to tell me what you see.

CAROLINE. *(Looking.)* I see two flies.

DR. DeLAMBRE. And?

CAROLINE. Well ... they're mating, Doctor. Shall I draw you a picture?

DR. DeLAMBRE. What *else* do you see?

CAROLINE. There is a third fly, buzzing above them. The other two are ignoring it.

DR. DeLAMBRE. All right. So there are three flies in this tank.

CAROLINE. Yes.

DR. DeLAMBRE. And two flies are female. The one buzzing alone. And one in the pair.

CAROLINE. All right.

DR. DeLAMBRE. The single male is eager to mate.

CAROLINE. How do we know this?

DR. DeLAMBRE. The male fly is *always* eager to mate.

CAROLINE. Naturally. And the female?

DR. DeLAMBRE. This one flying around is ready to lay ... oh, several hundred eggs.

CAROLINE. *(Pointing.)* But the male chose this one.

DR. DeLAMBRE. Well, yes and no. Look closely. Those two *aren't* mating.

CAROLINE. *(Looks closely.)* I don't understand. If they're not mating, what are they doing? I mean to say, if they're not mating, *why* aren't they mating?

DR. DeLAMBRE. Because this female is dead.

CAROLINE. She is? *(Looks. Realizes.)* She is! But the male —

DR. DeLAMBRE. Those two flies have mated before.

CAROLINE. What is he doing, then? Why isn't he with the other female? The live one?

DR. DeLAMBRE. Because he's mourning the dead one. He's remembering her. I believe that on some level — some primordial, cellular level — he's still in love with her. *(Short pause.)*

CAROLINE. Well, that's impossible. Insects don't *love*. They mate, they reproduce. Their nervous systems aren't developed enough for abstractions like love. A fly's consciousness ... Well, a fly *has* no consciousness. *(Digging into her bag.)* I — I just read an article about this — about insects' cognitive abilities — last night. Here, I brought it for you. There was a study done at the —

DR. DeLAMBRE. Thank you, Caroline. *(Caroline gives him the article.)* I hope that wasn't *all* you did.

CAROLINE. Pardon?

DR. DeLAMBRE. Read this article. I hope you did something else, something — fun. A young woman like you shouldn't —

CAROLINE. The study, Doctor, proposes that —

DR. DeLAMBRE. Did you go out last night with…?

CAROLINE. Doctor …

DR. DeLAMBRE. I'm asking casually.

CAROLINE. I *was* with Martin, Doctor. Yes.

DR. DeLAMBRE. Ah. And tonight, will you be — ?

CAROLINE. Yes. *(Pause.)*

DR. DeLAMBRE. I … Ah … *(Beat.)* My notes from last night …

CAROLINE. Of course, Doctor. *(The lights fade as Caroline goes to sit at her desk. New scene: Lights up on Dr. DeLambre. He sits hunched over a microscope. After a few moments, he looks up. The lab is empty. He checks his watch, looks towards the door, and returns to his work. A few more moments pass. Caroline comes in. Her right eye is swollen and bruised.)* Good morning, Dr. DeLambre. I'm late. I apologize.

DR. DeLAMBRE. *(Not looking up, all business.)* That's fine. I left you my notes by the typewriter. Could you — ?

CAROLINE. Of course, Doctor. *(They begin working. A few moments pass, then:)* How was your evening, Doctor?

DR. DeLAMBRE. Fine. *(They work in silence a few moments longer.)*

CAROLINE. Did you work late?

DR. DeLAMBRE. I did. I'm still on eyes. The fly's. And — yours.

CAROLINE. They're not much to look at this morning, I'm afraid. *(DeLambre looks at her, starts.)* I know how this must seem, Doctor, but please don't ask me about it. *(Definitely:)* It *won't* happen again. *(Pause.)*

DR. DeLAMBRE. Does it hurt?

CAROLINE. Yes.

DR. DeLAMBRE. May I put something on it?

CAROLINE. Doctor …

DR. DeLAMBRE. If you would like, I can put something on it for the pain. If you would like me to.

CAROLINE. I would, yes. *(Dr. DeLambre goes to a cabinet and picks out a bottle and cotton. He sits next to Caroline.)* Will it hurt, Doctor?

DR. DeLAMBRE. It won't, no. *(Gently, he dabs her eye with the medicine.)* This is caused … Do you know why this is caused? *(She shakes her head.)* This is caused by burst blood vessels. The capillaries just beneath your skin rupture, and blood spills out of them.

The blood collects and darkens into a purple pool. As it drains, the purple fades to blue, to yellow, to nothing …

CAROLINE. It feels cool.

DR. DeLAMBRE. It doesn't sting?

CAROLINE. No.

DR. DeLAMBRE. Good. *(Dr. DeLambre continues treating her black eye. The lights fade.)*

End of Play

INTERLUDE TWO

After "Insect Love" and before "The Ten-Minute Play about Rosemary's Baby." After the silence and darkness have been established, we hear the sound of flies buzzing as the lights come up to reveal M.T., swatting a fly with either a fly-swatter or a rolled-up horror comic book. After a few beats, he again notices the audience and starts jawing.

M.T. GRAVE. *(To audience.)* Will they get together — the young, nubile Caroline and the awkward, slightly uptight Dr. DeLambre? Or will their unspoken, unrequited, unconsummated, *Pinteresque* love remain — *horrors of horror* — hideously unfulfilled?

And what of the off-stage character Martin? Will Caroline be seeing him again? Will *we* ever get a gander? Will Dr. DeLambre? (What kind of name is "DeLambre" anyway?) Does anyone care? Anyone *awake* still? *(Looks around, checks the audience.)*

If you're not, kiddies, you'd better *perk up* and look *alive* — and look under your *seats* — because the Devil is in the house — Old Scratch himself — and the house is an apartment … a very, very *strange* apartment, in a very, very *strange* apartment building in New York City, overlooking Central Park … *(The stage around M.T. Grave starts to darken.)*

So settle back and say your prayers for the young married couple trapped in …

THE TEN-MINUTE PLAY ABOUT ROSEMARY'S BABY! *(M.T. Grave vanishes as a song like "Lullaby" from* Rosemary's Baby *starts to play.*)*

---

* See Special Note on Songs and Recordings on copyright page.

THE TEN-MINUTE PLAY ABOUT ROSEMARY'S BABY

CHARACTERS

The young couple:
BOY, a young man, an actor
GIRL, a young woman, his wife

The older couple:
MAN, Roman Castavet
WOMAN, Minnie, his wife

PLACE

A very strange apartment in the Bramford
building in New York City.

TIME

Summer, 1966.

With apologies to Mr. Ira Levin and Mr. Edward Albee.

THE TEN-MINUTE PLAY ABOUT ROSEMARY'S BABY

The stage is bare except for two oversized alphabet blocks and a Scrabble board downstage. The blocks are white and large enough for people to sit on them comfortably. One block has light blue accents; the other, pink. Note: The play should be brightly lit, except when the script calls for darkness. Then, it should be very, very dark.

As the play begins, a lullaby is playing and Boy and Girl are laughing, on their knees, playing Scrabble, tickling each other.

After a few moments, they start to kiss. And kiss. And kiss some more. Finally, embarrassed, they notice the audience and stop making out. They straighten their clothes — Boy is in a white T-shirt and jeans, Girl wears a pink sundress — and sit on their respective blocks. Boy and Girl are a young, attractive couple. Girl is blonde. They often speak to the audience.

BOY. Hi.
GIRL. Hello.
BOY. I'm Boy.
GIRL. I'm Girl. *(Big smiles. In unison:)*
BOY and GIRL. We *hate* our names —
GIRL. — but otherwise we're happy.
BOY. *(To audience.)* I'm an actor. *(Quickly.)* My character, Boy, is an actor. Boy's stage name is Guy.
GIRL. *(To audience.)* Guy's been in *Luther* and *Nobody Loves an Albatross*, and a lot of television plays and commercials.

BOY. *(To audience.)* We're invincible! Nothing can harm us! We never die! We live life to the fullest! *(Girl laughs.)* What? What is it? What's so funny, Girl?

GIRL. Nothing. Just … you're always hard, Boy.

BOY. Am I?

GIRL. Well, *aren't* you? Aren't you now? *(Boy shifts uncomfortably in his seat.)*

BOY. Don't you like it?

GIRL. Yes. I suppose. *(Considers it.)* No, I do. Yes. *(To audience.)* We just moved to New York. To a beautiful building overlooking the Park. The Bramford. Like the Dakota, but better.

BOY. Rent-stabilized. Southern exposures. Five and a half rooms — *(They smile, pleased.)* — and no one's ever been violently murdered there.

GIRL. Well, except for Steven Marcato, who practiced witchcraft and was torn to pieces by an angry mob in the lobby. And the Trench sisters, who ate babies. *(To Boy.)* And oh — don't forget that young woman I befriended in the laundry room in the basement. Terry … Something. She plunged to her death from a window. *(Beat.)* She was young. *(Beat.)* Like us.

BOY. I think there's a lesson in that. That sometimes … young people feel pain. That sometimes … young people suffer … are preyed upon … hurt.

GIRL. But not us? *(Short, nervous pause.)* Boy?

BOY. *(Noticeably ignoring her.)* So: This building — the Bramford — we love it. We love everything about it.

GIRL. Except for *them.*

BOY. Oh, they're not so bad. They're harmless.

GIRL. *(To audience.)* Our next-door neighbors. An older couple. *(Beat.)* One night, not long after we'd moved in, they invited themselves over for dinner. *(Man and Woman enter.)*

MAN. *(To Boy and Girl.)* Good evening, I'm Man.

WOMAN. Short for Ro*man.* Castevet.

GIRL. How do you spell that? Castevet?

WOMAN. C-A-S-T-E-V-E-T. Why, dear?

GIRL. Nothing. It just … sounds familiar to my ear.

WOMAN. Well, sure, it's that kind of name. I'm Woman, but please call me Minnie. *(To Man.)* Oh, Roman, look what they've done to the apartment. *(To Girl.)* Mrs. Gardenia, the previous tenant, was a dear old friend of ours until she mysteriously fell into a coma and died.

BOY. Really?

WOMAN. *(To Girl.)* How'd you think to arrange those blocks that way?

GIRL. Oh, I saw it in a magazine.

MAN. *(To Boy.)* Are you an actor?

GIRL. Boy's been in *Luther* and *Nobody Loves an Albatross* and a lot of television plays and commercials.

WOMAN. Well, that's where the money is, sure.

BOY. *(Grimly.)* Not to mention the artistic satisfaction.

MAN. Yes, *Luther*, of course. I knew I'd seen you in something. You had that wonderful gesture, that — You did a thing with your hand. You know.

BOY. Oh, you — you caught that?

MAN. Yes, very effective. It impressed me so much, I checked the program for your name. "Guy." I remember thinking: "A strong choice for such a young actor."

WOMAN. How old are you, Boy? *(Beat.)* Girl? *(Beat.)* Certainly old enough to have children, but — do you? Have children? *(Girl and Boy look at each other.)*

BOY. Not yet.

GIRL. Soon, we hope. We're very fertile, my family. All my sisters have babies. I'm one of eleven.

MAN. Of course. You're young yet.

GIRL. Please — sit. We'll get you drinks. Boy?

BOY. Coming right up! *(Boy and Girl exit. Man and Woman look at each other, then out to the audience.)*

MAN. *(To audience.) We came for their baby!*

WOMAN. Shh! Roman! Don't spoil it for them!

MAN. They won't tell. *(To audience.)* Will you?

WOMAN. She's … small-hipped, don't you think?

MAN. Shhh! Here they come again! *(Boy and Girl return, bearing glasses of strawberry blush.)*

GIRL. Ta-da!

WOMAN. Oh, Roman, look at that! Strawberry blushes!

GIRL. It was all we had on hand. We weren't expecting — company.

BOY. Girl …

MAN. We're intruding. We should go, Minnie.

WOMAN. Don't be ridiculous, Roman, we're not intruding, we're talking. This is what harmless, next-door neighbors do — they come over unexpectedly for chats. *(To Boy and Girl.)* Am I right, kids? *(Before they can answer.)* Say, Girl, you're not Catholic, are you?

GIRL. It's how I was raised, but now I don't know.

MAN. Boy, I wonder if we might have a word in private.

BOY. Sure! *(Man and Boy exit.)*

WOMAN. Where are you from, honey?

GIRL. Originally? From Omaha.

WOMAN. My goodness! What a change! Do you like New York?

GIRL. Now that we've found this lovely apartment.

WOMAN. Is it nicer than where you were living before?

GIRL. You have no idea. It was horrible. In Hell's Kitchen. I didn't feel safe at all.

WOMAN. And do you now?

GIRL. Do I now what?

WOMAN. Feel safe? Secure? Protected? Enough to — say — have a baby?

GIRL. I … *(Nervously, Girl looks offstage, to where Boy and Man went.)* What are they talking about in there, I wonder.

WOMAN. Why don't you have a baby — really?

GIRL. Well, Boy's career …

WOMAN. Comes first? *(Beat. Disapproving.)* Isn't that always the way?

GIRL. I … *(Man and Boy return. Boy is carrying another drink. It looks like a milkshake.)*

BOY. Ta-da! We're back! *(To Girl.)* And with another drink for you, sweetie!

GIRL. Oh, Boy, thank you. *(She drinks the drink, makes a face.)* Tastes funny. There's an … undertaste. A … chalky undertaste.

BOY. Don't be ridiculous, Girl, drink up! *(Girl does.)*

MAN. Well, we should be going, it's late.

WOMAN. Goodbye, children. Enjoy your evening. *(Man and Woman exit. Girl finishes her drink. Boy kisses her.)*

BOY. Girl … I want us to have a baby.

GIRL. Oh, Boy, do you mean it?

BOY. Right now. I'll get the lights. *(Boy exits, and the lights on the stage dim until only Girl's face is illuminated in a tight spot. Something like the creepy "Dream" music from* Rosemary's Baby *starts to play*.)*

GIRL. Something happened to me that night. The next morning, I'll find scratches on my back, on my side. "I wanted us to make a baby,"

---

* See Special Note on Songs and Recordings on copyright page.

Boy will say. "But … " I'll reply, "I dreamt I was raped by something inhuman." "Thanks a lot," he'll say. *(Beat.)* I dreamt … I saw in my dreams … yellow, demonic eyes, and there was a creature, making love to me, and Boy was there, and Roman, too, and I heard Roman say: *(Tight spot on Man, easily done with the actor holding a flashlight underneath his chin.)*

MAN. Boy, help her strip.

GIRL. And my clothes were torn off me and — and Boy, my lovely, young, hard Boy said: *(Tight spot on Boy.)*

BOY. She won't be hurt, will she? Promise me you won't hurt her. *(Tight spot on Woman.)*

WOMAN. She won't be hurt. We promise.

GIRL. I remember thinking: "This is no dream, this is really happening!" In the morning, I will ask: "What was that, Boy? Last night? What did you let them do to me?"

BOY. Shhh, baby, this is a dream. Tomorrow morning, you won't even remember it. *(To Man and Woman.)* She won't, will she?

WOMAN. Not if she drank the drink with the mouse in it, she won't.

GIRL. *(To audience.)* The letters C-A-S-T-E-V-E-T danced around in my head like Scrabble pieces. This part of the dream I will remember — later. The name … it's an anagram … The next morning, when I wake up, scratches on my back, I'll know: *(Lights snap up brightly. Girl is now visibly with child. To actors onstage:)* I'm pregnant. *(Man, Woman, and Boy cheer.)*

MAN. Congratulations, my dear.

WOMAN. Now this is good news! Look at you, honey, you're glowing!

MAN. Come, Minnie, let's let the children have their privacy. *(Man and Woman exit.)*

BOY. *(To Girl.)* Ma-ma …

GIRL. *(In response.)* Da-da …

BOY. Girl, I love you. *(Girl starts to cry.)* Oh, baby, what is it? What's wrong?

GIRL. I — I — I've been having this pain, Boy, I think there's something — I think there's something wrong with the baby.

BOY. Oh, now come on, Girl, there is nothing —

GIRL. That's not all. I think they're trying to hurt us.

BOY. Who?

GIRL. That older couple.

BOY. Why would they be trying to hurt us?

41

GIRL. Because … Because they're … Oh, Boy, I think they're witches and they want my baby!

BOY. Oh, now you're talking crazy!

GIRL. No, it's — *(Beat.)* That old man's name? Roman C-A-S-T-E-V-E-T? If you rearrange the letters, they spell — They're an anagram for Steven Marcato!

BOY. Who?

GIRL. Steven Marcato — the witch who was killed in our lobby! But he wasn't! That old man is Steven Marcato! Listen to me, Boy, I know how this sounds, but I read a book about witches and how they perform rituals — the witches, they're called covens, that's what they're called! — and they perform rituals with blood! And the most powerful blood is baby's blood! I think they've come for our baby because they're witches and they want our baby's blood. *(Pause. Stony silence from Boy.)* I know how that sounds, Boy, but we have to move! We do! They're evil. They want to hurt us.

BOY. You honestly expect me to believe that they're — That that harmless old couple — That they're witches? That in New York City, in 1966, that witches are real? And after our baby? Its blood?

GIRL. I know how it sounds …

BOY. We're not in any danger.

GIRL. How do — but how can you know?

BOY. Because, Girl, they promised me you wouldn't be hurt — *(Mini-beat.)* — and you won't be. *(Pregnant pause.)*

GIRL. *(Slowly, stunned.)* What was that, Boy? What did you say? *(Man and Woman enter, smiling.)*

MAN. Hello.

WOMAN. Good evening. Hi, Girl. *(With contempt.)* Boy.

MAN. It's time. We've come for the baby.

GIRL. You — you can't have it! You can't have its blood!

MAN. We don't want its blood, we want all of it.

GIRL. Boy, don't let them take our baby!

MAN. It's not Boy's baby, Girl, it's Satan's.

GIRL. What?

MAN. Satan is His Father, who came up from Hell and begat a Son of mortal woman!

GIRL. No …

WOMAN. *(To Girl.)* Yes. Satan chose you, honey. He brought you and Boy to this apartment here, He arranged everything that had to be arranged 'cause He wanted you to be the mother of His only living Son!

GIRL. Stop it. Stopitstopitstopitstopitstopitstopitstopitstop —

MAN. We've come for the baby — and we're not leaving without it.

BOY. *(To Man.)* Remember what you promised me. You promised me that she wouldn't be hurt.

MAN. But — she will be. You both will be.

GIRL. Boy?

BOY. *(Desperately.)* Why?

MAN. Because, children ... that's life. To be hurt. By others. *(Beat.)* By each other. *(Cataloging now.)* Betrayal. Deception. Cruelty.

WOMAN. To feel pain — to gain experience — to be hurt and have wounds —

MAN. A broken heart ... A loss of innocence ...

WOMAN. — whichever. To know that you are alive.

MAN. Do you understand?

BOY. No.

WOMAN. Girl?

GIRL. No. *(Quietly sobbing.)* Please don't ... *(Man and Woman start to converge on Boy and Girl.)*

WOMAN. Don't worry ...

MAN. ... you will ...

WOMAN. ... someday. *(Quick blackout. Fraught Silence.)*

End of Play

INTERLUDE THREE

After "The Ten-Minute Play about Rosemary's Baby" and before "Swamp Gothic": In the darkness, we hear a humming, and the lights come up to reveal M.T. Grave, holding a little baby in his skeletal arms.

M.T. GRAVE. *(Quietly singing.)* Hush little baby, don't say a word ... Daddy's gonna feed you a mocking bird ... *(Stops singing, starts cooing like an idiot.)* Ohhhhh, look how *cute* little Andy is! (That's his name, kiddies, *Andy*. Can you *stand* it?) Isn't he just *precious?* Don't you just want to *eat* 'im? Don't you just want to *gobble him up? (The baby makes a very loud "baby" noise. M.T. returns his attention to his bundle.)* Oh, looky-looky! Look who's waking up! How exciting! I'm all a-tingle 'cause I'm *finally* gonna get to see his beautiful baby-blue ... *(M.T. gasps, covers his mouth with his hand, looks around in horror like Mia Farrow does at the end of* Rosemary's Baby, *starts to shriek:)*

His eyes! What have you done to his eyes! And don't tell me he has his Father's eyes! I've met the Devil and the Devil's eyes look nothing like — THIS! *(With a flourish, M.T. Grave reveals "the baby," which is a stuffed doll with hideously crossed eyes — basically a doctored-up doll that looks totally absurd. He holds the doll up for a few beats, then pitches it offstage.)* That's enough baby-sitting for one night, I think. *(Brushes his hands clean of the doll.)* Besides, little Andy-Candy's not old enough to come with us where *we're* going next, kiddies. Which is the deepest, darkest, *muckiest* part of Louisiana. A foul, fetid, forgotten corner of marsh land called ... Blackwater. Bayou country, where unspeakable things — where *swamp* things, you might say — live ... *(An ancient, sonorous clock starts to toll the hour, pleasing M.T. to no end.)*

Ohohoh! Hear that? It's almost *tea time* at the Arcane family's decaying plantation — its *ancestral* mansion. Let's join them, shall we?

And maybe — just maybe — we'll get to see if home truly *is* where the heart is in ...

... *SWAMP GOTHIC!*

SWAMP GOTHIC

CHARACTERS

ALEC ARCANE, a nineteen-year-old Tulane student
ABIGAIL ARCANE, his sister
MATTHEW CABLE, his friend and lover

SWAMP GOTHIC

Lights up on a young man, Matthew Cable, in a dark, musty parlor. He wears a letterman's jacket and stands at the window, looking out into the night. He is handsome, with a strong jawline and broad shoulders and a body that looks best when it is slick with sweat, naked save for a white terrycloth towel wrapped tightly around his waist. He has the kind of body white terrycloth towels were intended for.

Outside, alligators are roaring. A terrible sound. A young woman walks in. She is pretty, and her hair — except for a single black streak — is white. Her hair has been that way for many, many years. She holds a stuffed pet alligator in her arms and strokes it inappropriately.

ABIGAIL. That's gator-speak for, "Sit down here, next to me."

MATTHEW. Gator-speak? You mean the —

ABIGAIL. Oh, yes, they talk. The gators, yes. Sing, too, at night sometimes. After they feed, in packs, like wolves.

MATTHEW. The — alligators, you're referring to?

ABIGAIL. We used to keep them as pets, my brother and I. We used to ride them like horses, holding onto a stick between their jaws — holding on for blessed life! Did you know that, Mister ... I've forgotten your name already.

MATTHEW. Matthew Cable.

ABIGAIL. Oh, yes. Ohhhh, yes. Of course it would be you. Who else would it be? Two years ago, my brother wrote me in a letter: "His arms are strong, Abigail, the veins on his arms stand out like steel cables. And that's his name, Cable." *(Beat.)* I thought, "Of all things for a man to notice ... his roommate's arms?"

MATTHEW. Matthew, if you prefer. Or Matt.

ABIGAIL. I do. *Matt.* You're a big hulking creature, aren't you,

Matt?

MATTHEW. I ... well ...

ABIGAIL. Do you play football, Matt?

MATTHEW. I don't.

ABIGAIL. Shame. I *adore* it. I adore its tedium. And its terrible, sudden, *brutal* violence.

MATTHEW. Ms. Arcane —

ABIGAIL. Abigail, please. *(Another gator roars. Abigail pats the empty seat beside her.)* Sit down here, next to me. *(Slowly, reluctantly, Matthew walks across the parlor and sits down next to Abigail.)* Would you like something to drink, Matt? May I offer you a mint julep? Some ... Southern Comfort, perhaps? I know you Tulane boys like to drink. Let me ring for a servant.

MATTHEW. I'm fine.

ABIGAIL. Perhaps you'd like a cigarette, then?

MATTHEW. Thank you, no.

ABIGAIL. Are you in training? I don't mean for football, I know that, but, perhaps you wrestle? Greco-Roman style?

MATTHEW. *(Sharply.)* Ms. Arcane, please. I'm trying to find your brother. Can you help me? Is Alec here? With your family?

ABIGAIL. My, my, my ... such *urgency* in your voice. Enough, Matt, that someone might mistake your urgency for passion.

MATTHEW. Your brother and I ...

ABIGAIL. My brother and you ... *what?*

MATTHEW. Your brother, Ms. Arcane, vanished from our fraternity house two weeks ago. In the middle of the night, in the middle of exams, without telling anyone, without leaving a note, without packing a single bag, he disappeared. We — me, his friends — we've looked everywhere. We want to know he's all right — that's all.

ABIGAIL. Ah, but then where are his other fraternity brothers? Where's that girl he writes to me about? What is her name? You must know it ... *close* as you are to my brother.

MATTHEW. Close? I ... I'm not entirely sure I know what you mean.

ABIGAIL. After all I've seen in these swamps ... do you really think I'd be shocked by anything you or my brother have done to each other — in the dark? In the heat? *(Beat.)* The Arcanes are an old family, Matthew, and I have many, many uncles. *(Short pause.)* As children, my brother and I shared a room for fourteen years. Fourteen years sleeping in the same room, so close I could reach out and grab him. There are no *secrets* in that kind of dark, Matt. My brother talks in his sleep.

MATTHEW. *(Significantly.)* I know. *(Short pause.)*

ABIGAIL. Well. Now we are getting somewhere. Yes, now we are. Perhaps now you'll even tell me about you and your ... predilections.

MATTHEW. Not just mine!

ABIGAIL. No?

MATTHEW. No. Your brother, too, he ... He showed me — no, he *taught* me ...

ABIGAIL. Yes? And *you*, Matthew? Were you a zealous pupil? When — and how — did your lessons begin? Tell it to me that way, as a story, if it's easier for you ... if it's more *palatable*. And if I approve of your story, if it pleases me, if it *satisfies* me, I'll tell *you* a story, too, about this terrible swamp that surrounds the Arcane family and its house. About how once, I had to destroy a man's idea of himself to save him.

MATTHEW. All I want to do is *see* Alec — !

ABIGAIL. You will. If he's here. And if I'm satisfied. *(Definitely:)* Afterwards.

MATTHEW. No. First, is he — ?

ABIGAIL. — I'll even get you started: "Your brother, Ms. Arcane, your dear, sweet, baby brother and I first met ... " When, Matthew?

MATTHEW. We met ... the winter of our first year at Tulane, right after Mardi Gras ... I woke up the morning after the last night of revels and stumbled through the haze of dawn and looked at the sun for the first time in days — in weeks! — and blinked the sleep from my eyes, and there was your brother, lying in the sun, on our porch swing, shirtless, his tan arm shading his eyes, pushing himself back and forth with one bare foot.

ABIGAIL. He showed up at your fraternity house? That's where you met?

MATTHEW. He was there to ... *collect* from one of my fraternity brothers.

ABIGAIL. Collect what?

MATTHEW. Payment for services tendered. *(Beat.)* Of course, I didn't learn of Alec's ... *inclinations* until much later. *(Beat.)* I was naïve, Ms. Arcane. Back then, I didn't even know that such things as your brother existed in this world.

ABIGAIL. My brother, too, was an innocent before he left

Blackwater.

MATTHEW. Blackwater?

ABIGAIL. The Arcane home, this house, is Blackwater, Matthew. Named for the river of black mud that surrounds it — the river of *ooze* that protects us from the outside world.

MATTHEW. Alec was like a vision from a dream that morning, Ms. Arcane. Alec and his dancer's body, Alec and his high cheekbones. That moment — that morning — remains frozen in my mind. In that instant, his beauty burned the fog of Mardi Gras from my mind. And the next moment, too — when he opened his slightly slanted lettuce-green eyes, and he looked at me, and he straightened himself up in that lazy way of his, and patted the empty place next to him on the swing and said: *(An alligator roars.)* "Sit down here, next to me," Alec said, and I did, and he kissed me —

ABIGAIL. !

MATTHEW. I *succumbed* to your brother's charms on that swing. So completely, in fact, that when he said, "Matt, let's go up to your bedroom," I agreed.

ABIGAIL. !!!

MATTHEW. We made *love,* Ms. Arcane. We made love until it was night again, and there was just moon in the room, and the curtains at my windows, stirring in the night breeze. *(Beat. He concludes:)* The next day, we went for a bike ride.

ABIGAIL. *(Hysterical.)* Liar! You've given yourself away! My brother has no bicycle! They were forbidden to us in Blackwater!

MATTHEW. The bicycle, Ms. Arcane, was mine. Alec rode its handlebars while I pedaled. That glorious day, I kept us balanced, as I would for the next year and a half, offering your brother a place in our fraternity house, settling up all his debts, protecting him from … *(Outside, silence.)*

ABIGAIL. Say it. Protecting him from what?

MATTHEW. From Blackwater. From whatever it is that goes on here. From —

ABIGAIL. What goes on here is our *business,* and our business is not just sugar and rice, though you saw our fields and our laborers, didn't you? *They* are our true business, our — *trade.*

MATTHEW. Alec's greatest fear, he told me, was to return home. It was why he supported himself the way that he did. He was *desperate* to never return here. He wanted nothing to do with you or this place or your business. He was happy — with me, at school.

He had friends. There was no reason for him to leave, but he did.

ABIGAIL. Because he had no choice *but* to return. Because stories of his ... *perversions,* his ... *indiscretions* trickled down to us, and we heard them, and the swamp *judged* my brother, and its judgment was a terrible thing, demanding ... *sacrifice.*

MATTHEW. ... sacrifice?

ABIGAIL. We'll have that drink now, shall we? *(She rings for a servant.)*

MATTHEW. I told you, I don't —

ABIGAIL. You will. After tonight, you will. *(A shuffling sound from beyond the parlor's door.)* That's Alec now, I think. *(Turning to the parlor door.)* Come in, Alec. *(Slowly, sonorously, the parlor door swings open. Slowly, more slowly than the door even, the thing that once was Alec Arcane, dressed as a house servant in a white coat and black pants, shambles in. There is dirt in his hair, underneath his fingernails. He is/was Matthew's age. Like Matthew, he was handsome and broad-shouldered, but now he's a thing of death ...)*

MATTHEW. *(Standing.)* Alec, thank God! Finally! *(Turns to greet him.)* Alec, baby, what are you doing here? *(Goes to him.)* We've been so worried. We all thought ... *(Closer to him.)* Why didn't you write ... or ... or call ... *(Stops moving.)* Alec? Alec, what is it? What's wrong?

ABIGAIL. He won't answer you, Mr. Cable.

MATTHEW. What are you talking about? *(Back to Alec.)* Alec? Alec, it's me, it's Matty. Alec, what is it?

ABIGAIL. *(To Alec.)* Alec, this man's name is Matthew Cable. He claims you were lovers. Is that true, Alec? Do you recognize this man, this Matthew Cable, as your lover? *(Slowly, with gravel and mud in his voice, Alec speaks. The blood chills at its sound.)*

ALEC. ... No ...

MATTHEW. What are you saying?! *(To Abigail.)* What have you done to him?

ABIGAIL. There is a certain procedure, Mr. Cable. A procedure that once performed cures one of — of consciousness. Of choice. Of *sin.*

MATTHEW. ... Consciousness?

ABIGAIL. Do you know what a "bokor" is, Mr. Cable?

MATTHEW. *(To Alec, close.)* Alec, it's me. It's Matt. Please ... answer me!

ABIGAIL. A bokor, Mr. Cable, is a voodoo priest, a practitioner of the dark arts, the … jungle arts.

MATTHEW. *(Turning to Abigail.)* What have you done to him?

ABIGAIL. The bokor, Mr. Cable — with juice from a puffer fish — poisoned my brother! And I buried him, and three days later — three days in the mud with the worms and the filth — the bokor brought him back! Reanimated him, but his mind — gone! His soul — gone! These parts of him you loved — gone and dead!

MATTHEW. But his body?

ABIGAIL. Lives on. Preserved and pumping, tireless. A drone, Mr. Cable, a zombie that exists only to work, to — to serve, to obey. *(Slowly, Matthew walks to Alec Arcane. He takes the thing's head in his hands and kisses it on the lips — long and hard. Matthew turns to Abigail. Shocked:)* Mr. Cable?!

MATTHEW. Whatever made you think it was more than his body I loved? *(Again, Matthew goes to kiss Alec. The lights fade.)*

End of Play

INTERLUDE FOUR

After "Swamp Gothic" and before "Morning Becomes Olestra." Darkness. Then a spot of light slowly rises on M.T. Grave, who sits off to the side of the stage, chomping on an enormous, bloody piece of lamb or drumstick. Or something like that. After a few moments of gorging himself, M.T. stops, notices the audience, and wipes his bloody chin.

M.T. GRAVE. Oh, I'm *SO* sorry, kiddies. How incredibly *RUDE* of me. How utterly *thoughtless.* Here I am, stuffing myself silly — enjoying a smorgasbord of slaughtered something or other — and there *you* are, sitting and wishing you'd had that extra slice of pizza before tonight's festivities …

Hmm … If only there were something I could give you … *(Thinks about.)* Wait a tick — what's *this* I feel squirming around in my pocket? *(Starts digging through his cloak.)*

Is it…? Could it be…? *(He pulls out a handful of writhing, fat, disgusting earthworms.)* Oh, no, that won't do at all, I'm afraid … *(Thinks some more as he starts chewing the earthworms absent-mindedly.)* Hmm … Ohhhh, *I* know …

Why don't I distract you with our evening's final offering: A cautionary tale guaranteed to take your mind off all things gastronomical. And, hopefully, convince you that *some* things are far, *far* worse than an empty stomach …

How does that sound, kiddies? *Appetizing* at all?

Well, then — pull up to the table for a blood-curdling yell-yarn, a heaping serving of hair-raising horror our producers *begged* me not to call …

… *MORNING BECOMES OLESTRA!*

MORNING BECOMES OLESTRA

CHARACTERS
(in speaking order)

M.T. GRAVE, a horror host

HAROLD HOGSWORTH, an enormous fat man

WANDA HOGSWORTH, his hot wife

AXEL, a refrigerator repairman (also a vampire, also hot)

MORNING BECOMES OLESTRA

Thunderclap. Lights up on a kitchen, where an enormous fat man, Harold, sits, polishing off the remains of his breakfast. At the sink, washing an enormous pile of dishes, is his wife, Wanda. It is dusk.

M.T. GRAVE. *(To audience.)* Meet Harold Hogsworth, kiddies. Four hundred-plus pounds of a grade-A white trash. *(Harold belches — a repulsive sound.)*

WANDA. Harold! God in heaven, you disgust me!

M.T. GRAVE. *(To audience.)* That's Harold's wife, Wanda. Whattya think, kiddies, a real looker, isn't she?

HAROLD. Aw, you love it. *(Harold belches again.)*

WANDA. Ugh! It's bad enough what you've done to your body — those massive folds of jiggling flesh, your little heart about to give out, your blubber-choked veins, your clogged intestines, your tiny, nearly invisible weenie — *must* you also make animal-like noises while you eat? It's grotesque!

HAROLD. Well, hell. If you're so unhappy, Wanda, why don't you divorce me?

WANDA. *(A gasp.) What?!* I've told you, Harold, I won't leave you while you're in this — this state. I won't do it. I — I love you too much.

HAROLD. Don't you mean you love *my money* too much?

WANDA. *(A gasp.)* What?! What kind of person do you think I am?

HAROLD. A low-down, scheming, money-grubbing slut who's after my pension. *(Beat.)* Hey, where's my lunch? *(Wanda pulls out an enormous suitcase — Harold's lunch.)* Thanks, Pork-chop. Hey, what kind of chips you put in?

WANDA. The — the regular kind.

HAROLD. You didn't try and slip me any of those fat-free chips again, didja?

WANDA. No, Harold.

HAROLD. Good. They make me wanna puke.

WANDA. Honestly, Harold. You know, if you tried, even a little, the cellulite would *melt* right off you. Why *not* eat fat-free Olestra potato chips every once in awhile?

HAROLD. I told you, Wanda, I won't have those things in my house. They give me — *(Stage whisper.)* — anal discharge. And slippery stool, too. It says so, right on the bag.

WANDA. God in heaven, Harold — *they're not Olestra chips!* Go ahead! Gorge yourself! Eat yourself to death for all I care! Now can we please have a civilized conversation? Please? For once?

HAROLD. Wish I could, Sweet-meat, but I'm late for work.

WANDA. *(A snort.)* Work. That's rich. Night watchman at a donut factory. Honestly, whoever heard of such a thing?

HAROLD. It puts bread on the table.

WANDA. It's *killing* me, Harold.

HAROLD. *(Rolling his eyes.)* Aw, shit.

WANDA. It is! You don't know! How could you? While you're here, sleeping the day away, languishing like — like the beached whale you are, I can't do any of my housework because it "disturbs you." So fine. So I try to rest when you rest. But then, at night, while you're at work guarding donuts, you expect me to function normally. I'm supposed to do all the shopping, run all the errands. Which is fine. Which I would do. Happily. BUT I CAN'T! Because everything in Morgansville closes at sundown! I haven't had a decent night's sleep since we were married!

HAROLD. Well, then, we're even. I haven't had a decent *fuck* since we were married!

WANDA. You disgusting beast! *(Wanda snatches up an iron skillet, raises it above Harold's head. Harold continues eating. The iron skillet remains poised. M.T. Grave steps forward.)*

M.T. GRAVE. I know what you're thinking, Wanda. One quick *whack!* and it would all be over. *(Beat.)* You can't do it, though, can you? Not because you haven't fantasized about it, God knows you have, but because you're scared of getting caught. A bloody frying pan ... there's no way you'd beat a murder rap. And besides, if you can just hold out a little longer ... Fat as he is, Harold's bound to *expire* any day now. Imagine that. Imagine what a nice, quiet life you'd be able to carve out for yourself on your widow's pension. *(Slowly, Wanda lowers the skillet.)*

HAROLD. Oh, and another thing, don't forget to get the refrigerator fixed.

WANDA. *(Sighs.)* Which one?

HAROLD. The one in the bedroom.

WANDA. And where do you expect me to find a repairman who works nights?

HAROLD. I'm sure you and your devious little mind will be able to come up with *something. (Harold gets up and exits, dragging his lunch behind him. Wanda returns to the sink and continues washing the dishes.)*

M.T. GRAVE. Careful with those dishes, Wanda, they were a wedding present … *(Wanda smashes the dishes in the sink, shattering them.)* … from Harold's mother. *(Wanda takes off her apron, dries her hands.)*

WANDA. Why won't he just *die? (From atop the refrigerator, she pulls a bag of WOW! potato chips. She eats one.)*

WANDA. Ummm-ummm! Absolutely nothing wrong with these Olestra chips. *(She eats another one.)* Anal discharge. A small price to pay … *(Next, Wanda pulls down a copy of the Yellow Pages. She starts to flip through them, all the while munching away on the chips.)* R … R … Railroads … R … R … Realtors … R … R … ah, Repairmen. Let's see … *(She reads.)* "Dead of Night Repair Service. When you need something fixed that can't wait till morning." *(Heading to the phone.)* Here goes nothing. *(She dials. They answer.)* Hello, Dead of Night Repair Service? *(They say something.)* Hi. I need something fixed that can't wait till morning. *(They say something else.)* A refrigerator. *(Something more.)* You can? *(One last thing.)* Well, of course you're invited. Honestly, what a silly thing to ask. My name is Wanda Hogsworth. Here, let me give you the address … *(The lights start to shift, indicating a passage of time.)*

M.T. GRAVE. Later that night, after Wanda has had her daily — oops, tee-hee — her *nightly* nightcap … *(A knock at the door. Wanda, slightly drunk, goes to open it. The repairman is there. He is tall, dark, and handsome. He is wearing an ordinary repairman's outfit, but there is nothing ordinary about him.)*

REPAIRMAN. Good evening, ma'am. *(Checks his work order.)* You Wanda Hogsworth?

WANDA. *(Sizing him up.)* Every inch of me.

REPAIRMAN. I'm here about a refrigerator …

WANDA. Of course. Won't you come in? *(He does.)*

REPAIRMAN. What seems to be the trouble?

WANDA. Well, for one, you haven't told me your name yet.

REPAIRMAN. Oh, it's Axel, ma'am.

WANDA. I'm Wanda. *(Sizing him up some more.)* And I can't tell you how long it's been since a man — a *real* man, I mean — has made love to me.

AXEL. *(Aw, shucks.)* I think that's a cryin' shame, ma'am, I truly do.

WANDA. It's my husband, Axel. He — he's a monster. You can't imagine. He weighs four hundred-plus pounds, he won't let me sleep, he's impotent, he's — he's obsessed with anal leakage. Honestly, I don't know how much longer I can bear it.

AXEL. Well, shucks. It's not my place to say, but why don't you leave him?

WANDA. He'd never give me a divorce. Oh, Axel, I haven't told you the worst part. He — he beats me.

AXEL. He does? Well, where's the abuser now?

WANDA. At work. Oh, Axel, I know I called about the refrigerator, but maybe you can help me fix this … *larger* problem.

AXEL. What can I do?

WANDA. Hold me. *(He does.)* Oh, how I've missed this. The feel of a real man pressed up against me. His broad shoulders, his chiseled chest, his veined arms, his semi-erect chubby poking my hipbone … If only this could be forever. If only I weren't married to Harold. If only after a night of passionate love-making I could persuade you to kill Harold for me …

AXEL. He's four hundred pounds?

WANDA. *Plus. (Wanda rips Axel's Dead of Night Repairman shirt away, revealing a chiseled chest. Wanda looks appreciatively to the audience over Axel's shoulder.)*

AXEL. Your bedroom?

WANDA. Through there. Would you like a drink first?

AXEL. No, thanks. I never drink … on duty. *(Wanda feels Axel's crotch.)*

WANDA. If this is a duty, you're certainly … *rising* to the occasion. *(Axel sweeps Wanda up in his arms. As he carries her off into the bedroom, M.T. Grave approaches the audience.)*

M.T. GRAVE. We'll skip the sex, kiddies, and *cut* straight to the violence. *(Wanda enters from the bedroom, sits down at the kitchen table.)*

The moon has gone down, it's a few minutes before dawn, and Wanda Hogsworth sits in her kitchen, awaiting Harold Hogsworth's return. What's that curling her lips? Can it be … a smile?

WANDA. *(Yawning.)* Finally! I'm going to be rid of my husband! After years of not being able to sleep for fear that his enormous girth would smother me, after years of waiting for him to die … *(She yawns again.)* My God, but that simpleton repairman's great in the sack. It's almost a shame I have to kill him. *(Trying out her story.)* "Oh, Officer, it was awful! Just awful! I don't know what happened. I came home from my morning jog and there was Harold — dead, with this strange refrigerator repairman standing over his body. I didn't know what to do and then he came towards *me* — as if to do me bodily harm — but luckily I had my registered revolver handy. Thank goodness my husband insisted I carry it with me at all times." *(Wanda gets up from the table and walks over to a cookie jar. She lifts its lid and pulls out a revolver. At that moment, Harold arrives.)*

HAROLD. Rise and shine, Pumpkin, I'm home! What's for dinner? I'm starved!

WANDA. *(Guiltily, as she quickly replaces the gun.)* Harold! I — I didn't hear you come in!

HAROLD. Apparently not. What's going on, Wanda?

WANDA. What do you mean?

HAROLD. I'm not blind, Baby-cakes, I see what's happening here. You're making to sneak a cookie, aintcha?

WANDA. A cookie? Oh. Oh, right. A cookie. Of course. *Ahhhh* … how was work, Harold?

HAROLD. Pretty good; we're trying out these new flavors. I gotta admit, I was pretty skeptical of honey-mustard-flavored donuts at first, but … truth be told, they ain't bad.

WANDA. Really? How … fascinating. *(Wanda replaces the jar's lid.)*

HAROLD. That revolver ain't loaded.

WANDA. I … I don't know what you mean.

HAROLD. It hasn't had bullets in it for the last six months. *(Short pause.)*

WANDA. But what if there's an intruder?

HAROLD. I'd be more worried about a desperate, sex-starved wife with crazy ideas in her head.

WANDA. *(After a short pause.)* That's not me, Harold … not anymore.

HAROLD. You're not desperate?

WANDA. Oh, no, I'm still desperate. I'm just not sex-starved any-more. *(Beat.)* It was savage, Harold. He fucked me twelve ways from Tuesday. We fucked on the bed, our bed, where there's a big hole because you're so fat, you impotent hog! We fucked on the floor like animals — like race horses in heat! We fucked here on this table! We fucked on top of your refrigerator — on *both* of them — and — it — was — *wonderful!*

HAROLD. Who?

WANDA. A man. A *real* man. A man who knows what it means to satisfy a woman. A man with a cock *this big* and balls *this round* and a stomach that's flat and — *and no bitch-tits!*

HAROLD. *You — dirty — tramp ... (Harold is approaching Wanda threateningly. Unafraid, she continues to taunt him.)*

WANDA. Me? *I'm* a dirty tramp? Because I have *needs*, Harold? Because I'm hungry? Because I am, Harold. *Hungry.* But not for food. Hungry for love! Hungry for affection! Hungry for sex. Hungry for contact with something that's maybe cheap and maybe sordid, but at least it's human, you fucking sow!

HAROLD. I'll kill you, you cunt. *(With surprising speed, Harold lunges at Wanda. He starts choking her.)* Die, you cunt! Die! Die!!! DIE!!! *(While Harold is choking Wanda, Axel enters the kitchen. Unnoticed by Harold, he comes up behind him, grabs Harold's hair ...)* Who — ? *(... pulls back Harold's head ...)* Who the fuck are *you* supposed to be? *(... and takes an enormous bite out of Harold's neck. Blood everywhere. On Axel, on Harold, on Wanda. Harold and Wanda are screaming. Axel starts lapping up Harold's blood.)*

WANDA. *(Kicking free of the men.)* Omigod! Omigod! Omigod! Omigod! Omigod! Omigod! *(Harold dies in Axel's arms. Axel con-tinues feeding, looks up at Wanda.)*

AXEL. *(Through his bloody mouth.)* Dead of Night Repair Service. When you need something fixed and it can't wait till morning.

WANDA. *(Gasping, choking.)* You're drinking his blood? But that means ... that means ... Oh my dear and holy God, it can't be, it's not possible, but ... you're a *vampire! (Axel continues feeding.)*

WANDA. Is he ... is he dead?

AXEL. *(Nodding.)* He — is — *dinner.*

WANDA. Thank God. But ... but ... What are you gonna do with me — Stud? *(Axel continues feeding.)* Axel? Lover? *(Beat.)* What about *me?*

AXEL. You? You, babe — are *dessert! (Axel tosses aside Harold's body as though it were a rag doll. Wiping his chin, he moves towards Wanda. Blackout.)*

End of Play

INTERLUDE FIVE

After "Morning Becomes Olestra" and before "Dinner with Super-Friends": As the lights on the tableaux go out, M.T. Grave is alone onstage, chomping on a donut. After a bite or two, he notices — guess what? — yes, ma'am, the audience!

M.T. GRAVE. You know something, kiddies? Say what you want about him, but Harold Hogsworth knows — or rather, he *knew* — his donuts! These honey-mustard ones *aren't* half bad ... *(He sneaks another big bite.)* Yum. Yep, not bad at all ... *(He finishes the donut, shakes the crumbs off his cloak, and claps his hands.)* Well, kiddies, I'm afraid that's all she wrote.

So join me tomorrow night for an entirely *different* and *new* assortment of fright-filled offerings, once more culled from the — *(Suddenly, the Stage Manager of* The Weird *appears, running down the aisle, towards our host.)*

STAGE MANAGER. Mr. Grave! Mr. Grave, sir!

M.T. GRAVE. *(Taken aback.)* Uh — yes?

STAGE MANAGER. Before you dismiss everyone, can I — um — hold on — I think maybe I should — *(He or she reaches M.T., whispers into his ear.)*

M.T. GRAVE. *What?* You can't be — *(Mini-beat.)* — surely you're not serious!

STAGE MANAGER. That's what they said ...

M.T. GRAVE. *Idiots!* But I'm M.T. Grave! I'm a *horror* host! I introduce *horror* stories, not — not — not —

STAGE MANAGER. — *Nevertheless*, payroll hasn't processed your check yet, so if you wanna get *paid* ...

M.T. GRAVE. Unbelievable. Would *[Insert rival theatre company's name here,]* do this, do you think? Would *[And another rival.]*?

STAGE MANAGER. Um, the actors are in their places, Mr. Grave.

M.T. GRAVE. All right — *fine. (The Stage Manager leaves, and M.T. Grave turns back to the audience.)* My apologies, in advance, but due to circumstances beyond my control, the powers that be

— our ever-so-thoughtful producers — have decided in their infinite wisdom that rather than end on a horrific note, they would like something a bit more ...

STAGE MANAGER. I believe the phrase used was "light-hearted, but still pulpy."

M.T. GRAVE. ... So although this presentation has been promoted and billed and enjoyed as an evening of horror playlets ... and although tales of mystery and the supernatural and the occult are my bread-and-butter — (Indeed, my *raison d'etre*.) — I am forced, begrudgingly, to cleanse your palate with yet one more story. Taken not from the *Haunt of Fear*, no, but from a magazine just to the left of it on the newsstand, a title — a place — called ... the *Hall of Justice*? (*A few chords of the theme music from the old* Super Friends *cartoon show begins softly, then grows ...)*

It's mealtime once again, kiddies, and you've been invited to have ... *DINNER WITH THE SUPERFRIENDS!*

DINNER WITH
THE SUPERFRIENDS

CHARACTERS
(in speaking order)

BIBBO, the ever-loving proprietor of Bibbo's Luncheonette, an older man with two kids.

FRANCES KANE, the superheroine formally known as Magneta; her friends call her Frankie.

SUPERGIRL, the world's most powerful teen superheroine, one of two survivors of the doomed planet Krypton; her real name is Kara, she looks — and will always look — seventeen.

Special tip o' the hat to Evan Dorkin and
Donald Margulies. (Thanks, guys.)

DINNER WITH
THE SUPERFRIENDS

*In the darkness, as the theme music from the old "Superfriends"
cartoon show winds down, the lights come up to reveal:*

*A table in a diner in front of a picture window that looks out
on the street. A young woman, Frances Kane, sits at the table,
having a coffee and reading a novel. After a few moments, she
checks her watch. Someone's late. An older man, the owner of
the coffee shop, Bibbo, walks by with a pot of coffee.*

BIBBO. *(To Frances.)* You want some more coffee, Frankie?
FRANCES. Ahhh … *(Checks watch again.)* No, thanks, I should
probably wait. Thanks, Bibbo.
BIBBO. 'S no problem, Frankie. I'm the same way myself. Too
much coffee, and I'm *moon*-bouncing offa the walls. *(Bibbo starts to
head for the kitchen, stops, turns back.)* Hey, Frankie, I'm dyin' to
ask: How come you're friends with her? I mean, I know you're a
bigshot doctor and everything, don't get me wrong, but — I mean
— she's … Well, you know … She save your life or something?
FRANCES. Actually … yeah. She did, yes. And I … I've helped
her out a couple of times. *(Beat.)* It's hard to explain …
BIBBO. I hear ya, I hear ya, I don't mean to pry, I was just asking
… Well, I'll just be over there, waiting patiently …
FRANCES. She'll show up. Trust me. *(Bibbo moves away, to wipe
down his counter. Frances returns to her novel. After a few moments,
there's a tapping on the picture window. Frances looks up. It's the
world's greatest teen heroine: Supergirl! When she smiles, it's like a ray
of pure sunlight, which makes sense since Supergirl, like her older
cousin Superman, is a living solar battery. Frances and Supergirl wave
to each other through the glass. For a moment — just a second, really*

— Supergirl's expression clouds. Frances doesn't catch it. Supergirl comes into the restaurant.)

SUPERGIRL. Frankie!

FRANCES. *(Standing.)* Hey, you! *(They hug. It's pretty wonderful. Once, they were best friends.)*

SUPERGIRL. I'm *SO* sorry I'm late!

FRANCES. Oh, God, don't worry about it, I'm just — *(Spontaneously, the two friends hug again, shrieking and laughing.)* Is this your new costume? It's fabulous! *(Supergirl twirls.)*

SUPERGIRL. Do you love it?

FRANCES. I love it, I do.

SUPERGIRL. I can't believe you hadn't seen it before.

FRANCES. Well, I had — in magazines — but it's stunning! I love your little cape. Look at you!

SUPERGIRL. Thanks. *(As she sits:)* Wonder Woman hates it!

FRANCES. Oh — whatever — she does not.

SUPERGIRL. No, she does! She says it's offensive.

FRANCES. To whom?

SUPERGIRL. Exactly.

FRANCES. God, she gets to fight crime in a one-piece with an American eagle across her —

SUPERGIRL. *Thank* you —

FRANCES. But whenever anyone else —

SUPERGIRL. I know, it's ridiculous.

FRANCES. You hungry?

SUPERGIRL. Oh, my God — STARVING!

FRANCES. Great! One second and we'll — *(Frances turns to call for Bibbo, but he's already there with menus.)* Oh, hi, Bibbo, can we — ? *(He hands them menus. Bibbo can't take his eyes off Supergirl. Somebody pinch the man, he's dreaming.)* Oh, thanks.

SUPERGIRL. *(As she studies her menu.)* God, everything looks so — What's good here?

BIBBO. *(Still looking at Supergirl.)* Uhhhhhhh …

SUPERGIRL. Why don't I start with the … meatloaf … and a plate of spaghetti and meatballs with an extra order of — *(To Frances.)* How are the mashed potatoes?

FRANCES. Great. Like clouds, they're so fluffy.

SUPERGIRL. *(Finishing her order, to Bibbo.)* And an extra side of mashed potatoes. And a vanilla milkshake. And a root beer float. And onion rings. *(She gives him her menu.)* Thank you.

BIBBO. You're, ah … That is, it's my, uhm … Uhhh …

FRANCES. Can I get the hamburger platter, too, Bibbo, but can I get a salad instead of mashed potatoes?

BIBBO. Uhhh … sure.

FRANCES. Great. And a —

SUPERGIRL. Get a milkshake.

FRANCES. And a Diet Coke, please. *(To Supergirl.)* Says the girl with the super-metabolism.

BIBBO. *(Writing down the order.)* And … one … Diet Coke. You got it.

FRANCES. Great. Thanks, Bibbo.

SUPERGIRL. Yeah, thanks!

BIBBO. I'll just, ah, put this order in. Then I'll just be … You know, if you need anything else …

FRANCES. We'll let you know. Thanks, Bibbo.

BIBBO. … Right. *(Bibbo moves away from their table, towards the kitchen. Supergirl and Frances look at him, then at each other. They both laugh; Frances shakes her head.)*

SUPERGIRL. He's great!

FRANCES. Oh, yeah, he's a doll.

SUPERGIRL. I love this place! God, I can't think when the last time I had a real meal in a real diner was!

FRANCES. I'm sure. The first thing I did when I quit — well, after throwing away that ridiculous costume — was eat a double-bacon cheeseburger.

SUPERGIRL. I still can't believe you actually went through with it — quitting.

FRANCES. Some days — bad days — I wake up sometimes and I look around my house — or I'm in my office, and it's late at night, it's nine or ten, and nothing's gone right the entire day — and I wonder: "What was I thinking?"

SUPERGIRL. What *were* you thinking? Fighting crime, hanging out in space, saving lives … How do you turn your back on that?

FRANCES. I still save lives, Kara.

SUPERGIRL. You know what I mean.

FRANCES. Listen, being a doctor maybe isn't the flashiest profession, but *really:* What did I *do* as Magneta? Seriously — what *could* I do? Tap into the Earth's electromagnetic energies? Manipulate them? And do what? Bend metal? Magnetize objects? I mean, what *is* that?

73

SUPERGIRL. You miss it. I *know* you miss it.

FRANCES. Well … of course I do. But I'd never go back.

SUPERGIRL. People say that, and they probably — I'm sure they think it, too, and believe it, but —

FRANCES. I wouldn't. It's all so different now, so … creepy. *(Beat.)* These new villains? I read about them, Kara, I try to keep up, but I swear to you: I don't get them. How they work, why they do what they do … It used to be fun … The Hall of Justice, the Legion of Doom … The bad guys got the best lines and the coolest toys, but we always won … Now … they're just *evil. (She shakes her head.)* Anyway — how's this new guy? This "new" Green Lantern?

SUPERGIRL. Who, Kyle?

FRANCES. I guess he's not new anymore. New to me. God, new superheroes … They're like New Coke. No one really likes them, do they? Have you ever noticed that? Why is that?

SUPERGIRL. No, they do. Now they do. Kyle's all right. He's young. Immature.

FRANCES. He cute?

SUPERGIRL. Yes. *(Thinks about it.)* Yes — very. He's got that — You know, his hair flops down into his eyes, in front of his mask. *(Beat.)* They're *all* cute, Frances, they're like TV actors that way.

FRANCES. God, *aren't* they? *(Beat. Frances leans in.)* So, are you — ? How about you, are you seeing anyone?

SUPERGIRL. Oh, God, Frankie, what do *you* think?

FRANCES. Well, how should I know? I don't know, I think that new Green Arrow's pretty attractive. What's his name? Connor Something?

SUPERGIRL. What are you *talking* about?

FRANCES. You don't think he's cute? With that little goatee?

SUPERGIRL. Frankie, Connor's — Green Arrow's gay.

FRANCES. What?

SUPERGIRL. Uh-huh. He's dating Plastic Man's son — Elastic Boy. Superman doesn't say much, but I don't know … I think they're good role models for kids. And they're happy. Listen, they're the most stable superhero couple I know.

FRANCES. Good for them. *(Short, fraught pause.)*

SUPERGIRL. Frankie … I want to give you something. And ask you a favor.

FRANCES. Sure, but — I mean — shouldn't *I* be giving *you* a gift?

SUPERGIRL. It's a pretty big deal …

FRANCES. Okay ... *(Supergirl hands Frances a small metal box. Frances takes it, shakes it.)* What's in it? *(She starts to open the box. Supergirl clamps the box's lid down. Tight.)*

SUPERGIRL. No, don't do that. Don't open it while I'm here.

FRANCES. *(Nervous smile.)* Kara ... what's going on?

SUPERGIRL. Do you remember the story of how I got my powers? How I'm not really from Earth, but from a planet in another galaxy?

FRANCES. Krypton. (Of course, I saw that "Behind the Heroes" special on VH1.)

SUPERGIRL. The same planet Superman came from. Our parents sent us off in separate rocket ships just before Krypton exploded.

FRANCES. And you both crash-landed here on Earth. And it's the yellow sun that gives you your powers, right?

SUPERGIRL. That's what Superman thinks ... *(Looks away.)* Oh, Frankie ...

FRANCES. Kara, what is it? What's wrong?

SUPERGIRL. When Krypton exploded, pieces of it fell to Earth — like meteors. Which are green — which glow green. Kal — Superman — he calls them kryptonite. *(Beat.)* They're the one thing on Earth that can kill us. Radiation from them ... *(Pause. Frankie looks at Supergirl, then at the box she's just been given.)*

FRANCES. I don't want it, Kara. *(She pushes it away.)* What would I possibly want with it?

SUPERGIRL. Frankie ... if something happens to me, if I start ... hurting people, I want someone to be able to stop me.

FRANCES. What are you talking about? Why would you start hurting people?

SUPERGIRL. It's happened before. Sometimes ... sometimes, heroes go bad, Frankie, you know that.

FRANCES. Okay, but why me? I'm not even — I mean, it's not like I'm even a superhero anymore.

SUPERGIRL. If someone broke in to rob this place right now, you're telling me you'd sit by and watch it happen? *(Frankie doesn't say anything.)* If I turn ... evil, I want the power to stop me to be in the hands of the person I trust more than anyone else on the planet. Even Superman. *(Pause.)* You're my best friend, Frankie.

FRANCES. Kara ...

SUPERGIRL. Promise me, all right?

FRANCES. ... Okay. *(Short pause.)* Okay, I will — I do — I

promise.

SUPERGIRL. … Thank you. *(The two friends look at each for a few moments, neither knowing what to say. Thankfully, Bibbo comes over to their table, loaded down with plates of food.)*

BIBBO. All right, ladies, soup's on!

SUPERGIRL. Great! I'm starved!

FRANCES. Oh, my goodness. Look — *(Still uncomfortable with things.)* — look at all this …

SUPERGIRL. What are you talking about? This is a snack for me. Pass the ketchup, will you? *(Supergirl stops suddenly, cocks her head to one side.)*

FRANCES. *(Ketchup bottle in hand.)* Kara? What is it?

SUPERGIRL. Do you hear that?

FRANCES. Hear what? I don't hear any —

SUPERGIRL. *(Matter-of-factly.)* No, of course not, you don't have super-hearing. It's the Justice League Distress Signal. *(Listens some more.)* Oh, dear; apparently Gorilla Grodd's tearing apart Central City. *(Beat.)* Again.

FRANCES. If it isn't Mirror Master, it's Gorilla Grodd …

SUPERGIRL. I *hate* that this always happens …

FRANCES. No, it's okay, I understand. Go, go. Just …

SUPERGIRL. Yeah?

FRANCES. … Just stay safe, okay? *(Supergirl flashes that smile. Her super-smile.)*

SUPERGIRL. Always. *(Starts to go, stops, turns back.)* Call me!

FRANCES. I will. *(Waves.)* See you next year, Kara.

SUPERGIRL. Wild horses couldn't stop me! *(Winks.)* Later, alligator! *(With that, Supergirl strides out the door, Bibbo right behind her. Through the window, we see Bibbo look up into the sky — as we hear the WHOOSHING! sound of someone taking off.)*

FRANCES. Bye, Kara … *(Frances is alone in the diner. She sits at her table.)* … and happy birthday. *(The lights begin to fade. As they do, Frances picks up the small metal box. She opens it. Whatever's inside does, indeed, glow green. The lights fade completely to black and all we see is the green glow of the kryptonite. After a few moments, that goes away, too.)*

EPILOGUE

After "Dinner with the Superfriends." As Frankie closes the lid on the kryptonite, a spot comes up on M.T. Grave, dabbing his eyes with a red handkerchief.

M.T. GRAVE. Awww ... Now doesn't that just make your insides go all warm and gooey like a stinking, fetid, steaming bucket of entrails? *(Suddenly:)* Oh, which reminds me ... *(From behind his chair, M.T. Grave lifts a red, splattered bucket. He reaches into it and pulls out a handful of ... stinking, fetid, steaming entrails.)* What's left of our *pulchritudinous producer* after the little chat we just had backstage ... *(He shrugs.)* What can I say? We parted over artistic differences, then *I* parted *him* — *(Mini-beat.)* — *with a machete!* *(He cackles.)*

So on that note — and no more teasing this time, kiddies, I promise — why don't we bring our evening's journey into the unknown to a screeching halt, *hmmmmm?*

And come back again soon, won't you? *(He starts to exit, stops, turns back to the audience.)*

And tonight ... when you get home ... before you turn off the lights and slip under your covers ... don't forget to check under your beds or in your closets ...

You never know what weird thing or other might have followed you home ... *(M.T. Grave bows to the audience and turns to go — this time completely turning around — so we see that someone's taped a "KICK ME" sign on his back. Thunder, lighting, creaking as M.T. Grave leaves the stage, cackling.)*

The Ever-Loving End!

PROPERTY LIST

BLOODY MARY
Lipstick, purse
Bloody knife

INSECT LOVE
Microscope, notes, pen
Typewriter
2 lunch bags with sandwiches
Sheet, mask
Books
Article, purse
Notes
Watch
Bottle and cotton

INTERLUDE TWO
Fly swatter or rolled up comic book

THE TEN-MINUTE PLAY ABOUT ROSEMARY'S BABY
2 Large alphabet blocks
Scrabble board
Strawberry blush drinks (2)
Milkshake

SWAMP GOTHIC
Stuffed alligator
Bell for servants

INTERLUDE FOUR
Bloody drumstick or lamb shank
Earthworms

MORNING BECOMES OLESTRA
Breakfast food, dirty dishes
Apron
Suitcase with lunch food
Iron skillet
Bag of chips
Yellow Pages
Phone
Cookie jar
Revolver
Stage blood

INTERLUDE FIVE
Donut

DINNER WITH THE SUPERFRIENDS
Cup of coffee, novel, watch
Pot of coffee, dishcloth
Menus
Order pad and pen
Small metal box
Plates of food
Ketchup bottle

EPILOGUE
Red hanky
Red splattered bucket with entrails

SOUND EFFECTS

BLOODY MARY
Ominous chord
Radio Announcer

INTERLUDE ONE
Thunder, lightning
Ominous underscoring

INTERLUDE TWO
Buzzing of flies

INTERLUDE THREE
Baby noise
Clock tolling

SWAMP GOTHIC
Alligators' roar
Shuffling sound

MORNING BECOMES OLESTRA
Thunderclap

DINNER WITH THE SUPERFRIENDS
Tapping on window
Whooshing sound

EPILOGUE
Thunder, lightning
Creaking

NEW PLAYS

★ **GUARDIANS by Peter Morris.** In this unflinching look at war, a disgraced American soldier discloses the truth about Abu Ghraib prison, and a clever English journalist reveals how he faked a similar story for the London tabloids. "Compelling, sympathetic and powerful." *–NY Times.* "Sends you into a state of moral turbulence." *–Sunday Times (UK).* "Nothing short of remarkable." *–Village Voice.* [1M, 1W] ISBN: 978-0-8222-2177-7

★ **BLUE DOOR by Tanya Barfield.** Three generations of men (all played by one actor), from slavery through Black Power, challenge Lewis, a tenured professor of mathematics, to embark on a journey combining past and present. "A teasing flare for words." *–Village Voice.* "Unfailingly thought-provoking." *–LA Times.* "The play moves with the speed and logic of a dream." *–Seattle Weekly.* [2M] ISBN: 978-0-8222-2209-5

★ **THE INTELLIGENT DESIGN OF JENNY CHOW by Rolin Jones.** This irreverent "techno-comedy" chronicles one brilliant woman's quest to determine her heritage and face her fears with the help of her astounding creation called Jenny Chow. "Boldly imagined." *–NY Times.* "Fantastical and funny." *–Variety.* "Harvests many laughs and finally a few tears." *–LA Times.* [3M, 3W] ISBN: 978-0-8222-2071-8

★ **SOUVENIR by Stephen Temperley.** Florence Foster Jenkins, a wealthy society eccentric, suffers under the delusion that she is a great coloratura soprano—when in fact the opposite is true. "Hilarious and deeply touching. Incredibly moving and breathtaking." *–NY Daily News.* "A sweet love letter of a play." *–NY Times.* "Wildly funny. Completely charming." *–Star-Ledger.* [1M, 1W] ISBN: 978-0-8222-2157-9

★ **ICE GLEN by Joan Ackermann.** In this touching period comedy, a beautiful poetess dwells in idyllic obscurity on a Berkshire estate with a band of unlikely cohorts. "A beautifully written story of nature and change." *–Talkin' Broadway.* "A lovely play which will leave you with a lot to think about." *–CurtainUp.* "Funny, moving and witty." *–Metroland (Boston).* [4M, 3W] ISBN: 978-0-8222-2175-3

★ **THE LAST DAYS OF JUDAS ISCARIOT by Stephen Adly Guirgis.** Set in a time-bending, darkly comic world between heaven and hell, this play reexamines the plight and fate of the New Testament's most infamous sinner. "An unforced eloquence that finds the poetry in lowdown street talk." *–NY Times.* "A real jaw-dropper." *–Variety.* "An extraordinary play." *–Guardian (UK).* [10M, 5W] ISBN: 978-0-8222-2082-4

DRAMATISTS PLAY SERVICE, INC.
440 Park Avenue South, New York, NY 10016 212-683-8960 Fax 212-213-1539
postmaster@dramatists.com www.dramatists.com

NEW PLAYS

★ **THE GREAT AMERICAN TRAILER PARK MUSICAL music and lyrics by David Nehls, book by Betsy Kelso.** Pippi, a stripper on the run, has just moved into Armadillo Acres, wreaking havoc among the tenants of Florida's most exclusive trailer park. "Adultery, strippers, murderous ex-boyfriends, Costco and the Ice Capades. Undeniable fun." *–NY Post.* "Joyful and unashamedly vulgar." *–The New Yorker.* "Sparkles with treasure." *–New York Sun.* [2M, 5W] ISBN: 978-0-8222-2137-1

★ **MATCH by Stephen Belber.** When a young Seattle couple meet a prominent New York choreographer, they are led on a fraught journey that will change their lives forever. "Uproariously funny, deeply moving, enthralling theatre." *–NY Daily News.* "Prolific laughs and ear-to-ear smiles." *–NY Magazine.* [2M, 1W] ISBN: 978-0-8222-2020-6

★ **MR. MARMALADE by Noah Haidle.** Four-year-old Lucy's imaginary friend, Mr. Marmalade, doesn't have much time for her—not to mention he has a cocaine addiction and a penchant for pornography. "Alternately hilarious and heartbreaking." *–The New Yorker.* "A mature and accomplished play." *–LA Times.* "Scathingly observant comedy." *–Miami Herald.* [4M, 2W] ISBN: 978-0-8222-2142-5

★ **MOONLIGHT AND MAGNOLIAS by Ron Hutchinson.** Three men cloister themselves as they work tirelessly to reshape a screenplay that's just not working—*Gone with the Wind.* "Consumers of vintage Hollywood insider stories will eat up Hutchinson's diverting conjecture." *–Variety.* "A lot of fun." *–NY Post.* "A Hollywood dream-factory farce." *–Chicago Sun-Times.* [3M, 1W] ISBN: 978-0-8222-2084-8

★ **THE LEARNED LADIES OF PARK AVENUE by David Grimm, translated and freely adapted from Molière's *Les Femmes Savantes.*** Dicky wants to marry Betty, but her mother's plan is for Betty to wed a most pompous man. "A brave, brainy and barmy revision." *–Hartford Courant.* "A rare but welcome bird in contemporary theatre." *–New Haven Register.* "Roll over Cole Porter." *–Boston Globe.* [5M, 5W] ISBN: 978-0-8222-2135-7

★ **REGRETS ONLY by Paul Rudnick.** A sparkling comedy of Manhattan manners that explores the latest topics in marriage, friendships and squandered riches. "One of the funniest quip-meisters on the planet." *–NY Times.* "Precious moments of hilarity. Devastatingly accurate political and social satire." *–BackStage.* "Great fun." *–CurtainUp.* [3M, 3W] ISBN: 978-0-8222-2223-1

DRAMATISTS PLAY SERVICE, INC.
440 Park Avenue South, New York, NY 10016 212-683-8960 Fax 212-213-1539
postmaster@dramatists.com www.dramatists.com

NEW PLAYS

★ **AFTER ASHLEY by Gina Gionfriddo.** A teenager is unwillingly thrust into the national spotlight when a family tragedy becomes talk-show fodder. "A work that virtually any audience would find accessible." *–NY Times.* "Deft characterization and caustic humor." *–NY Sun.* "A smart satirical drama." *–Variety.* [4M, 2W] ISBN: 978-0-8222-2099-2

★ **THE RUBY SUNRISE by Rinne Groff.** Twenty-five years after Ruby struggles to realize her dream of inventing the first television, her daughter faces similar battles of faith as she works to get Ruby's story told on network TV. "Measured and intelligent, optimistic yet clear-eyed." *–NY Magazine.* "Maintains an exciting sense of ingenuity." *–Village Voice.* "Sinuous theatrical flair." *–Broadway.com.* [3M, 4W] ISBN: 978-0-8222-2140-1

★ **MY NAME IS RACHEL CORRIE taken from the writings of Rachel Corrie, edited by Alan Rickman and Katharine Viner.** This solo piece tells the story of Rachel Corrie who was killed in Gaza by an Israeli bulldozer set to demolish a Palestinian home. "Heartbreaking urgency. An invigoratingly detailed portrait of a passionate idealist." *–NY Times.* "Deeply authentically human." *–USA Today.* "A stunning dramatization." *–CurtainUp.* [1W] ISBN: 978-0-8222-2222-4

★ **ALMOST, MAINE by John Cariani.** This charming midwinter night's dream of a play turns romantic clichés on their ear as it chronicles the painfully hilarious amorous adventures (and misadventures) of residents of a remote northern town that doesn't quite exist. "A whimsical approach to the joys and perils of romance." *–NY Times.* "Sweet, poignant and witty." *–NY Daily News.* "Aims for the heart by way of the funny bone." *–Star-Ledger.* [2M, 2W] ISBN: 978-0-8222-2156-2

★ **Mitch Albom's TUESDAYS WITH MORRIE by Jeffrey Hatcher and Mitch Albom, based on the book by Mitch Albom.** The true story of Brandeis University professor Morrie Schwartz and his relationship with his student Mitch Albom. "A touching, life-affirming, deeply emotional drama." *–NY Daily News.* "You'll laugh. You'll cry." *–Variety.* "Moving and powerful." *–NY Post.* [2M] ISBN: 978-0-8222-2188-3

★ **DOG SEES GOD: CONFESSIONS OF A TEENAGE BLOCKHEAD by Bert V. Royal.** An abused pianist and a pyromaniac ex-girlfriend contribute to the teen-angst of America's most hapless kid. "A welcome antidote to the notion that the *Peanuts* gang provides merely American cuteness." *–NY Times.* "Hysterically funny." *–NY Post.* "The *Peanuts* kids have finally come out of their shells." *–Time Out.* [4M, 4W] ISBN: 978-0-8222-2152-4

DRAMATISTS PLAY SERVICE, INC.
440 Park Avenue South, New York, NY 10016 212-683-8960 Fax 212-213-1539
postmaster@dramatists.com www.dramatists.com

NEW PLAYS

★ **RABBIT HOLE by David Lindsay-Abaire.** Winner of the 2007 Pulitzer Prize. Becca and Howie Corbett have everything a couple could want until a life-shattering accident turns their world upside down. "An intensely emotional examination of grief, laced with wit." *–Variety.* "A transcendent and deeply affecting new play." *–Entertainment Weekly.* "Painstakingly beautiful." *–BackStage.* [2M, 3W] ISBN: 978-0-8222-2154-8

★ **DOUBT, A Parable by John Patrick Shanley.** Winner of the 2005 Pulitzer Prize and Tony Award. Sister Aloysius, a Bronx school principal, takes matters into her own hands when she suspects the young Father Flynn of improper relations with one of the male students. "All the elements come invigoratingly together like clockwork." *–Variety.* "Passionate, exquisite, important, engrossing." *–NY Newsday.* [1M, 3W] ISBN: 978-0-8222-2219-4

★ **THE PILLOWMAN by Martin McDonagh.** In an unnamed totalitarian state, an author of horrific children's stories discovers that someone has been making his stories come true. "A blindingly bright black comedy." *–NY Times.* "McDonagh's least forgiving, bravest play." *–Variety.* "Thoroughly startling and genuinely intimidating." *–Chicago Tribune.* [4M, 5 bit parts (2M, 1W, 1 boy, 1 girl)] ISBN: 978-0-8222-2100-5

★ **GREY GARDENS book by Doug Wright, music by Scott Frankel, lyrics by Michael Korie.** The hilarious and heartbreaking story of Big Edie and Little Edie Bouvier Beale, the eccentric aunt and cousin of Jacqueline Kennedy Onassis, once bright names on the social register who became East Hampton's most notorious recluses. "An experience no passionate theatergoer should miss." *–NY Times.* "A unique and unmissable musical." *–Rolling Stone.* [4M, 3W, 2 girls] ISBN: 978-0-8222-2181-4

★ **THE LITTLE DOG LAUGHED by Douglas Carter Beane.** Mitchell Green could make it big as the hot new leading man in Hollywood if Diane, his agent, could just keep him in the closet. "Devastatingly funny." *–NY Times.* "An out-and-out delight." *–NY Daily News.* "Full of wit and wisdom." *–NY Post.* [2M, 2W] ISBN: 978-0-8222-2226-2

★ **SHINING CITY by Conor McPherson.** A guilt-ridden man reaches out to a therapist after seeing the ghost of his recently deceased wife. "Haunting, inspired and glorious." *–NY Times.* "Simply breathtaking and astonishing." *–Time Out.* "A thoughtful, artful, absorbing new drama." *–Star-Ledger.* [3M, 1W] ISBN: 978-0-8222-2187-6

DRAMATISTS PLAY SERVICE, INC.
440 Park Avenue South, New York, NY 10016 212-683-8960 Fax 212-213-1539
postmaster@dramatists.com www.dramatists.com